…suppose a Man was carried asleep out of a plain
Country amongst the Alps, and left there upon the Top
of one of the highest Mountains, when he wak'd and
look'd about him, he wou'd think himself in an enchanted
Country, or carried into another World; every Thing
wou'd appear to him so different to what he had seen or
imagin'd before.
To see on every Hand of him a Multitude of vast Bodies
thrown together in Confusion, as those Mountains are;
Rocks standing naked round about him; and the hollow
Valleys gaping under him; and at his Feet, it may be,
an Heap of Frozen Snow in the midst of summer.

Burnet, *Sacred Theory*, I, 191-192

Two climbers on the southern flank of Snow Dome

III

Ice cave, Stutfield Glacier   Stutfield Glacier terminus

Glacier flour etched by frost   Athabasca River

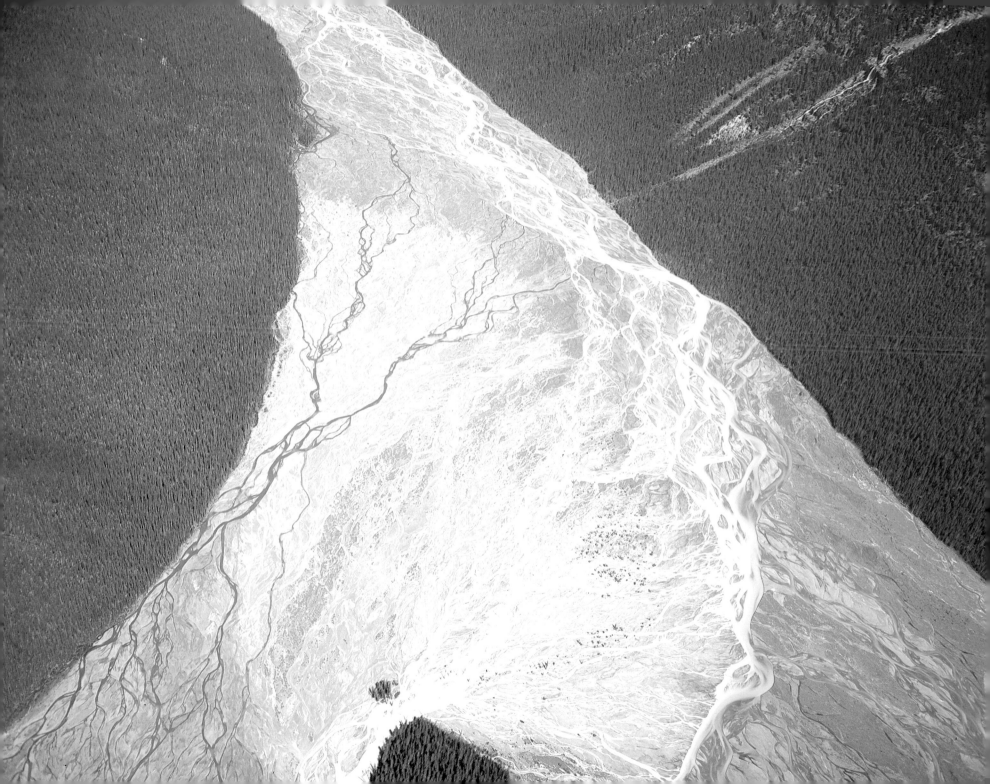

Striated rock

Unnamed glacier
south of Wales Glacier

VIII

Crevasses, Snow Dome; Mount Andromeda rises behind

COLUMBIA ICEFIELD
A SOLITUDE *of* ICE

ACKNOWLEDGEMENTS

The authors would like to express the gratitude to the following individuals and institutions for permission to reproduce or quote materials as noted below.

The Archives of the Canadian Rockies, Peter and Catharine Whyte Foundation, Banff, Alberta for permission to reproduce the historical photographs, pp. 62, 66, 68, 71, 73, 74, 81, 83, 85 & 89

The Corporate Archives of the Canadian Pacific Railway for permission to reproduce the colour photograph on p. 88

Mr. Rick Kunelius for permission to reproduce the colour photograph on p. 83

Loren Eiseley, *The Star Thrower*, 'The Winter of Man', Copyright© 1978 by the Estate of Loren C. Eiseley, reprinted by permission of Times Books, a division of Quadrangle/The New York Times Book Co., Inc.

Ronald Clark, *The Victorian Mountaineers*, quoted with the permission of B.T. Batsford Ltd., London

J.S. Collins, *The Vision of Glory*, quoted with the permission of Penguin Books, London

Robert Sharp, *Glaciers*, quoted with the permission of The University of Oregon Press, Eugene

for Norah
who never knew precisely what the authors were doing out there in the world of ice

First published in 1981 by Altitude Publishing Ltd.
box 490, Banff, Alberta, Canada, T0L 0C0
ISBN 0-919381-00-6
Printed and Bound in Canada
Published in the United States of America in 1981 by The Mountaineers,
719 Pike Street, Seattle, Washington 98101
ISBN 0-89886-035-0
Library of Congress Catalogue Card No. 81-80257
THE MOUNTAINEERS: Organized in 1906 "…to explore, study, preserve, and enjoy the natural beauty of the Northwest."

CONTENTS

Athabasca Glacier environs; from left: Mount Athabasca, Mount Andromeda, Athabasca Glacier, Snow Dome, Dome Glacier

PREFACE

ONE ADVANTAGE TO BEING neither a professional historian nor naturalist is the freedom to tell a good story simply. *Columbia Icefield: A Solitude of Ice* is a short, informal account of the natural and human history of the Canadian Rockies' Columbia Icefield. Documentation and cross-referencing are minimal and I have substituted a suggested reading list for a multi-page bibliography.

The text is divided into three sections: a basic discussion of glaciers in general, a tour of the Columbia Icefield, and a human history of the Icefield environs. For those new to the world of glacier ice, a brief glossary has been included at the end of the book for easy reference.

Glaciology, despite the best efforts of many very dedicated individuals, is an unconsolidated discipline. Had I given equal space to all the theories explaining any given phenomenon, or footnoted all the definitions existing for any one feature, I would have written exactly the sort of technical treatise I wish to avoid. Therefore, after reading through several dozen sources and taking copious notes on such wonderfully delectable (and obviously deletable) topics as *transverse sublacustrine varve counts,* I settled on four or five publications covering the ground I was interested in and accepted whatever they had to tell me. Whenever these sources were at odds I chose either the explanation or definition supported by the majority, or, that failing, whichever appealed to me most.

My basic sources, then, for the natural history section, were Robert P. Sharp's *Glaciers* (Eugene, Oregon: University of Oregon Press, 1960), Austin Post and Edward R. LaChapelle's *Glacier Ice* (Seattle: University of Washington Press, 1971), and two publications of the Canadian Inland Waters Directorate. *Glacier and Landform Features in the Columbia Icefield Area, Banff and Jasper National Parks, Alberta, Canada,* is a two volume report with supplemental maps written for Parks Canada by the Glaciology Division of the I.W.D. and dates to March, 1978. Compiled by S. Baranowski, W.E.S. Henoch, and R.E. Kucera, it is an excellent source for anyone interested in the portions of the Icefield falling within Parks Canada jurisdiction. On the problem of glacier classifications I turned to Inland Waters' Glacier Inventory Note No. 4, *Information Booklet for the Inventory of Canadian Glaciers.* Compiled by C. Simon Ommanney, the booklet is an invaluable aid to anyone lost in the morass of contradictory classification systems.

The section on human history was more straightforward. If I felt any story was more than fifty percent untrue I indicate as much; otherwise I have honoured the traditions of Rocky Mountain yarn swapping. Most of the sources are listed in the suggested reading list.

I would like to acknowledge several individuals who assisted me with this project: Ted Hart, Director of the Whyte Foundation's Archives of the Canadian Rockies, and his staff, for research assistance; C. Simon Ommanney, head of Environment Canada's Perennial Snow and Ice Division, for pointing me in the right direction; Ron Perla, also of Environment Canada, for suggestions relating to some of the technical aspects of "Understanding Glaciers" F.O. "Pat" Brewster, Dorothy Cranstone, Ken Jones, and Maryalice Stewart for their remembrances of days past; Jon Whyte, for extensive editorial assistance; and Susan Beckett, my wife, for her patience.

A man who keeps company with glaciers comes to feel tolerably insignificant by and by. The mountains and glaciers together are able to take every bit of conceit out of a man and reduce his self-importance to zero if he will only remain within the influence of their sublime presence long enough to give it a fair and reasonable chance to do its work.

Mark Twain, *A Tramp Abroad*

SEEN FROM THE PRAIRIES, the Rocky Mountains of Canada form a ragged, shining interweaving of rock and sky rising above the foothills to the west–a dancing, glittering, erratic electrocardiogram of a line tracing the heartbeat of those observing for the first time.

From Calgary, it's only a little over an hour's drive to the shadows of the Rockies, and if first-time mountain visitors are impressed with the view from the prairies, they are inevitably awestruck as they enter a foreign and forbidding vertical world. A few suffer claustrophobia, threatened by the sudden intimacy of soaring rock faces, knife-edged ridges, and crenulated, glacier-wreathed summits; but the common reaction is more akin to intoxication, an immediate and euphoric response to what romantic poets have long considered the alpha and omega of natural scenery.

For those who would pursue the heart of these mountains, there is no better place to spend time than the Columbia Icefield, an immense, exotic slab of shifting blue ice sprawling across the Great Divide at the border of Banff and Jasper National Parks. As a topographical entity, the Icefield is the geographic and hydrographic apex of North America, the point from which all land falls away and delicate feathers of snow yield bright drops of water to three oceans; as a mountain presence, the Icefield and its circumglacial peaks crystallize the Rocky Mountain moods and meanings.

The Icefield distills the mountains. Prodigiously powerful and ominous in the way only mountain phenomena can be, it possesses a magnitude and potential violence to reduce an individual to meaninglessness. Imbued with a primeval sense of monumental beginning, it is a fresh, heady place of extreme contrast; at once a wild, tangled corner of the world where thousands of thousands of tonnes of ice stir, groan, split, and collapse, and a grand arena of continually changing light, vibrant colour, intricate pattern, rich texture, and complex form. Desolate and beautiful, it is a topography to define the word wilderness.

Most mountain travelers, unless blessed with the peculiar instincts and capabilities of a mountaineer, see but one small fragment of the Columbia Icefield. Reduced by mountain landscape to tiny beads of colour, the visitors stand at the toe of the Athabasca Glacier, little realizing it is but one of nearly thirty such glaciers which tumble down from a far vaster solitude of ice lying hidden above. Yet, for most, if the Athabasca is only a teasing intimation of what lies beyond the mountain wall, it is still quite enough to raise fundamental and disquieting questions concerning man's true place in the natural world.

Like all mountain phenomena, the Icefield demands the experience of the senses. Why else would thousands of tourists each year brave the cold glacier winds and the rains of August just to put a hand on the Athabasca tongue? Is it by touch we comprehend an object so alien to our everyday existence? Or, perhaps, begin to find the origins of our uniquely human life? There is a magic here, a sense of the unknown, a mystery which eludes definition, and it draws us to it, seeking contact with something lost beneath the façade of our urban twentieth century lives.

UNDERSTANDING GLACIERS

The glaciers creep
Like snakes that watch their prey, from their far fountains,
Slow rolling on; there, many a precipice,
Frost and the Sun in scorn of mortal power
Have piled: dome, pyramid, and pinnacle,
A city of death, distinct with many a tower
And wall impregnable of beaming ice.

Shelley, *Mont Blanc*

Mount King Edward
from the south

UNDERSTANDING GLACIERS

G LACIERS BLANKET CLOSE TO ELEVEN PERCENT of the earth's land surface (down from over thirty percent not so many thousand years ago). They anchor approximately seventy-five percent of the planet's fresh water in frozen reservoirs. They influence the climates of significant portions of the world. They have shaped much of the globe's face. They provide keys to unlock some secrets of the earth's past. And, although today glaciers are suffering an interlude of general decay, we can believe they will return to a former prominence someday in the future. It is wise, then, to learn of them today, before, some bright and startling morning, a glacier tongue starts lapping at the garden gate. Why are there glaciers? What makes an icefield? Good questions.

Glaciers are complex beasts, their parts and processes tricky to pin down, and they demand intellectual perseverance from those who would wish to know them. Even the experts have their difficulties: one noted glaciologist has observed that the controversies about what glaciers are and how they move have generated enough heat to melt a small one. Fortunately, the fundamentals are not difficult to grasp: common sense applied to common experience can illuminate a glacier's component parts and basic processes, and the rest we may leave safely to academic hairsplitters. Coefficients of friction, the mechanisms of crystallographic deformation, and the specifics of interferometry depth sounding need not concern us here.

THE BASICS

When most people think of a glacier, which is probably not frequently, they visualize a bare, blue wedge of ice of unspecified proportions which may or may not have deep fissures texturing its surface. It is, they know, both cold and dangerous. It is interesting to note, as a first step toward an expanded glacier consciousness, that a wide variety of glacier types exists, ranging from polar ice caps hundreds of kilometres across and thousands of metres thick, to tiny, isolated glacierets often mistaken for snow patches. Each is classified by criteria such as overall form, source of nourishment, longitudinal profile, temperature, and degree of activity. We'll begin by defining one or two types and move on to others as the need arises.

So: what, indeed, is a glacier? Simply defined, it is a perennial body of ice which forms in those regions of the world where more snow accumulates than melts or evaporates. The peaks of the Canadian Rockies, with their northerliness, high altitudes, and harsh climate, qualify collectively as one such region.

An *icefield** is a mass of ice which has the appearance of a sheet or blanket, and reflects, in form and flow, the irregularities of its underlying topography. Nourished by seasonal snowfall and by snow avalanching onto its surface from overlooking mountain summits, an alpine icefield typically develops in a lofty basin or on a high plateau where accumulating snow slowly transforms into ice. Over the course of many years–decades, and centuries–the ice builds in size and weight until its own increasing bulk animates it. The margins of the icefield begin to bulge and buckle. Ponderous, frozen tentacles slowly extend from the mothering mass and begin a slow crawl along passages of least resistance toward the valleys below. Any such stream of ice issuing from an icefield is termed an *outlet glacier;* one moving down a well-defined valley is an *outlet valley glacier.*

Because we perceive its movement and changing form, we think a glacier is living and anthropomorphize it in commonly used glaciological terms. A glacier's catchment area, for instance, is its head; the terminus its toe, or foot, or snout; the glacier surface its face; the separate ice streams of a divided glacier its arms; and the main body of a valley glacier its tongue. A man alone on a glacier, it is said, will eventually hear its tongue tell a story.

The advance of a glacier tongue is a convincing, menacing ex-hibition of natural force. The encroaching ice shears off, as if they were twigs, ancient trees a metre or more in diameter; it sweeps away boulders as if they were grains of sand; it temporarily dams or diverts whole rivers. A glacier's progress may not be rapid–a few centimetres to a few metres a day**–but it is as inexorable as time itself.

The advance is also, for the glacier tongue that perhaps dreams darkly of encircling the globe, an exercise in futility, for as the tongue advances from its high mountain cradle and begins its descent, it encounters a lower, progressively warmer climate and begins to melt. The lower it descends, the more it melts, and the progress, which began with such vehemence and determination in the cold highlands, falters: the glacier's march weakens, fails, and the ice thins to a knife edge and disappears.

It follows from the foregoing description that a glacier is composed of two principal parts: an *accumulation zone,* in which more snow accumulates than melts over the course of a year, and provides material for the tongue's advance, and a *wastage,* or *ablation zone,* in which more snow melts than accumulates, and serves to check the tongue's progress. In the late summer the two zones can be easily identified: the lower part of the glacier displays the dark, milky, exposed ice of the wastage zone, while in the accumulation zone white, unmelted snow blankets the upper part of the glacier.

Throughout the winter the entire glacier lies mantled in snow, but as the strong spring sun begins to claim snow from the lower portions of the glacier, a ragged edge appears between the exposed ice and the unmelted snow, a discontinuity called the *snowline.* It is an ephemeral feature which advances up the glacier as the summer pro-

*The major glaciological terms used in this book are defined in the glossary at the end of the book.

**Occasionally a glacier, for as yet unexplained reasons, will "surge" or "gallop," and will achieve impressive velocities. In 1973, for example, the Black Rapids Glacier in Alaska suddenly began to advance at 75 metres a day, and some glaciers in the Himalayas have been clocked at close to 120 metres a day. The Columbia Icefield has yet to produce a galloping glacier, and a film producer has yet to use the idea for a disaster movie.

gresses. At autumn's onset, however, the line reaches a maximum elevation, usually about 2850 metres in the Rockies. Once it has established its highest position for the year the snowline becomes the *annual snowline* and, since it is such a highly visible feature, it is an obvious, if only approximate,* delineator of the accumulation and wastage zones.

Snow accumulation is the prime mover of glaciers, and a glacier's state of well-being depends, to a large degree, on the balance of snow accumulating and snow melting. Glaciers characteristically strive to dispose of exactly as much snow as they acquire each year. Glaciologists refer to the phenomenon in terms of an "annual budget," and at least one, Robert Sharp, observes that glaciers balance their snow budgets much better than most governments do their financial ones. According to Sharp,

> If a deficit occurs [lower than average snow accumulation], the glacier contracts in order to decrease expenditures. If the glacier experiences a surplus, it promptly expands in order to dispose of this additional income. It abhors both surplus and deficit, and does its level best to live exactly up to its income.

In any given year, in a relatively stable meteorological environment, accumulation may exceed wastage slightly, or melt exceed the previous winter's snowfall, but over the course of five to ten years the balance will be very close.

THE NATURE OF ICE

The ice of glaciers is transformed snow, and the metamorphosis from snow to ice begins as soon as the delicate, porous flakes reach earth. Partial melting, sublimation, and compaction usually destroy the feathery spikes of the snowflakes in a day or two, leaving small granu-

*For several reasons beyond this book's scope the precise balancing line between annual snow accumulation and wastage lies slightly below the annual snowline. Glaciologists refer to it as the *equilibrium line*.

lar spheres of "old" or "corn" snow which nestle closely together. In circumstances of low temperature, high humidity, and little wind, however, the weathering can extend to many weeks.

Soon successive layers of new snow cover the old and the weight of the overlying accumulation further crushes, compacts, and modifies the snow's structure. In a year's time it becomes *firn* or *névé,* an intermediary substance between snow and ice in which the separate granules of old snow have to some extent joined together. When melting, refreezing, recrystallization, compaction, and realignment of the firn advances to the point that the pores between individual grains are sealed into bubbles which do not interconnect, or "communicate," true glacier ice emerges, a hard, dense, granular polycrystalline mineral, impermeable to both air and water, bearing little resemblance to the frothy stuff of a dry snowfall.

One of the physical properties of ice, its impermeability, makes each glacier an atmospheric archive. As the firn fuses into a single body it entombs air, pollen, dust, and other motes of atmospheric debris. Since the ice deep in a glacier may date back several hundred years, the entrapped material presents a sample of the earth's atmosphere as it was before man began to tinker with it. The amount of enclosed air also helps determine the colour of the ice: ice containing a high percentage of air bubbles appears white and opaque, while ice which has had most of its air squeezed out is transparent, smooth, and blue.*

It is incidental but interesting to note the lengths to which people have gone to describe an obviously fascinating element. Since the

*"Why is the ice blue?" Generations of tour guides and park naturalists have answered the question: "If you were that cold, you'd be blue, too!" In fact, the ice crystals and particles of dust within them act as prisms, absorbing the long wave colours penetrating the ice to depth; and reflecting the short wave colours–the blues and greens. The colours are most vivid in ice which is pure and unmodified–as seen in crevasses and ice caves–while surface ice, much modified by evaporation and melt, and carrying an overburden of dirt and pollen, reflects the entire spectrum of light and appears white. Air bubbles also reflect all of the visible light.

Polished ice; ice cave, Athabasca Glacier

first study of glaciers, about 150 years ago, both scientist and poet have struggled gamely for an apt comparison. What substance does glacier ice approximate? A quite serious and vituperous argument rumbled throughout the universities of Europe in the latter 1840's and early 50's concerning the nature of ice. John Steward Collings, in *The Vision of Glory*, describes it:

> Ten years' wrangling and quibbling over the word 'viscous' and the word 'plastic' and the word 'elastic' and the word 'malleable' and the word 'ductile'; and dispute as to whether ice is more like ice-cream than treacle, or putty than glue, or lava than wax, or clay than butter, or jam than jelly....

The Romantic poets, who had discovered the delights of nature earlier in the century, and who considered mountains the beginning and end of all scenery, gave themselves apoplexy searching for metaphors, a tradition undiminished to the present. No less a personage than the poet Marianne Moore suggests "glass that will bend," while wilderness writer and crack cynic Edward Abbey, at a less romantic remove, trains his jaded eyes at "blue streams of snot."

Most of us prefer Moore's expression, but it comes no closer than Abbey's, for glacier ice most closely resembles, in describing the truth of the matter, rock. Sedimentary in origin, metamorphosed by pressure, glacier ice is essentially rock with a low melting point. It is an attribute which continues to enamour geologists: why journey to the centre of the earth to study what's happening a few yards from the road?

GLACIER MOVEMENT

In the flow of ice is the glaciers' magic. In their alternating advances and retreats we find both fascination and reason for bestowing living attributes. We also find, in these icy waxings and wanings, contradiction enough to befuddle the senses. How could anything so grandiose

as a block of ice large enough to fill a valley be in motion? An ice cube, left to its own devices, just doesn't wander off.

Neither does glacier ice–as we have seen–until it meets certain prerequisites. Not until the ice reaches a depth of approximately thirty-three metres does it assume certain plastic qualities, a function of its accumulated weight. Given the critical thickness and the tug of gravity, the ice begins to deform and flow. The tilt of the rock beneath the ice determines the direction or directions of flow, and the gradient of the bedrock determines, in large part, the velocity of flow. The steeper the gradient and the thicker the ice, the faster the flow.

The actual mechanics of glacier flow, like the description of the nature of ice, have been cause for metaphorical concern among glaciologists. Just how and why do those white dragons dance as they do? Is the flow an extruding flow: toothpaste from a tube? A sliding flow: beans sliding across each other in a bean bag? A liquid flow: molasses from a barrel? A sleigh down a hill? At present two commonly accepted theories account for most movement measured in any given glacier. One has to do with "basal slippage," in which the glacier as a whole, lubricated by meltwater, slides over its bedrock base; the other is a more complicated process involving adjustments and movement within individual ice crystals. The degree of flow attributed to each process varies from glacier to glacier.

The pattern of glacial flow, less of a mystery, is easily observed. When Agassiz, Charpentier, Forbes, and Tyndall, the fathers of glaciology, first proved glaciers move, they also demonstrated that the velocity of flow varies from one part of a glacier to another. By setting a series of metal stakes across the tongue of the glacier under consideration and recording the stakes' progress downslope, the naturalists learned that most valley glaciers, in a fashion similar to rivers, flow more rapidly in their middles than at their sides, where friction with valley walls and the thinning of ice reduce speed. Later generations of glaciologists, inserting long pipes vertically into a glacier and later measuring the amount each pipe was bent during encasement, determined that glaciers generally move more rapidly toward their surface than at their base. The actual velocities vary greatly, from glacier to glacier, and from place to place and even from time to time on the same glacier.

GLACIER FEATURES

A rudimentary knowledge of what glacier ice is and how it moves makes it easier to understand, if not anticipate, some of the major features of a glacier. Most are quite conspicuous, and the ability to identify even a few of them can foster an appreciation for and impart sense to what otherwise appears a chaotic natural event.

Crevasses. It has been estimated that 30,000 crevasses transect the surface of Athabasca Glacier alone. Crevasses are simply fissures in the ice surface formed under the influence of various strains, but their formidable appearance and nasty habit of swallowing the unwary has earned them respect in the folklore of various places of the world. To many North American native peoples crevasses were the abode of the most abhorrent of evil spirits. For a handful of lost, snowblind and demoralized men trying to find their way across Malaspina Glacier to the Klondike goldfields in 1898, crevasses were the home of horrific monsters which reached up to pluck away members of the group one by one. For certain Victorian adventure writers and novelists (from whom we have inherited many of our notions) they were maneaters which gobbled up stout-hearted men and were thus incidentally responsible for the vapours suffered by the women at home.

Not the best press, but partially justified. Crevasses are intriguing, beautiful, and a little bit dangerous. Many reach depths of forty metres, are metres wide, and can stretch across the width of a glacier. Sheer, sharp, and often undercut, they drop precipitously into cold, dark, and dripping places most people would prefer to avoid. They are guaranteed to be absolutely no fun should one stumble unroped at the brink.

However, should a slip occur, there is cold comfort in knowing history may not be finished with the victim. In 1820, on the Glacier des Bossons below Mont Blanc in the Alps, an avalanche caught and hurled five climbing guides into a deep crevasse. Of the five, two were rescued and three were lost. Forty-three years later recognizable bits of body and equipment began to appear at the glacier snout and one of the surviving guides, now an old man, was able once again to shake hands with the climbing companion of his youth.* J.D. Forbes, who studied the glacier some twenty years after the accident and, among other things, measured its velocity, predicted within a year the date the deceased men would begin to melt out.

Glaciers at depth are very malleable, readily willing to flow with the lay of the land. Their upper surfaces, however, do not bear the weight of any overlying ice and remain brittle and subject to cracking. Since different sections of a glacier move at varying velocities, the pressures where two flow patterns intersect are great. Crevasses appear wherever those pressures exceed the tensile strength of the ice's fragile upper mantle. Most valley glaciers, for example, display a series of crevasses along their margins: the differing rates of flow between the central and marginal ice literally tear the surface of the transition zone into elongate cracks.

Crevasses, then, are a function of differential ice flow, and flow, in turn, is a function primarily of bedrock topography and gradient. Where the bedrock is smooth and of shallow slope the glacier flow is regular and little crevassing occurs. Where the bedrock is gnarled

*Mark Twain, in *A Tramp Abroad*, has a marvellous account of this story, along with other amusing glacier tales.

and steep, however, the flow is highly irregular and the glacier's surface is tortured.

The extent of crevassing and the arrangement of the crevasses* mirror the underlying bedrock. Their depth, on the other hand, is limited solely by the depth of the glacier's brittle mantle. Since the ice is highly pliable only within thirty metres of the surface it is a rare crevasse that is more than forty metres deep.

Two particular types of crevasses merit special mention. The first is the *bergschrund*. Ice often forms on the rock walls cradling a glacier, but, if the rock is too steep or windswept, it never reaches the critical depth necessary for flow. A bergschrund is the long, jagged, semi-permanent crevasse which appears wherever the moving ice of a glacier encounters such an apron of stationary ice. Bergschrunds are most frequently seen at the heads of alpine glaciers, separating the thin, immobile layer of ice adhering to the valley headwall from the glacier itself.

During the late summer, when a season of full sun has melted out the winter's drifted snow, bergschrunds can be massive clefts, the objects of vehement abuse from climbers attempting to reach a summit ridge from a glacier approach.

The second is the *randkluft* to which the term *bergschrund* is frequently and erroneously applied the break appearing between moving ice and bare rock; this rift, is caused by the warmth of the dark rock melting adjacent ice and has little to do with differential flow.

Icefalls. Wherever a glacier moves over a cliff-like incline in the bedrock, an *icefall* is generated. As in a waterfall, the descending material greatly accelerates and the ice stretches and weakens. The result is one of the true glories of mountain scenery, an anarchistic turbulence of unbridled potency, equal parts ruptured ice and raw energy. Crevasses and ice twist and buckle and intersect, constantly rearranging themselves and creating three and four storey high, teetering blocks and spires of ice. Most of these *seracs* slip down the icefall in a more-or-less orderly fashion, but many, torn from their moorings, slowly tip, turn and collapse, toppling in ruin against other pillars only slightly more stable, playing a game of dominoes with ice cubes the size of box cars, accompanied by detonations which would shame a howitzer. A large icefall, 750 metres to a kilometre high, is a thunderous display of power, of never-ending fascination to an observer.

Below an icefall, the ice compresses back together, the glacier reconstitutes itself; crevasses and seracs disappear as the bedrock evens out, and the ice moves on down the valley, rearranged but very much intact.

Meltwater. The wastage zone of a glacier is the region of melting snow and ice lying below the equilibrium line, and it is logical that the *meltwater* a glacier produces contributes a few interesting wrinkles to its structure. Wrinkle is a fitting term, for the most obvious meltwater feature is the myriad of streams which courses a glacier's face, each cutting its own bed in the ice. Such streams can etch the entire surface of a glacier into a continuous series of swells and swales with a relief varying from as little as several centimetres to a metre and more.

---

*One common method of classifying crevasses is by their orientation to the long dimension of the glacier tongue–*transverse, longitudinal,* or *oblique*–and by their location on the glacier–*marginal, central,* or *terminal.* Thus might one find transverse terminal crevasses, or oblique marginal crevasses, etc.

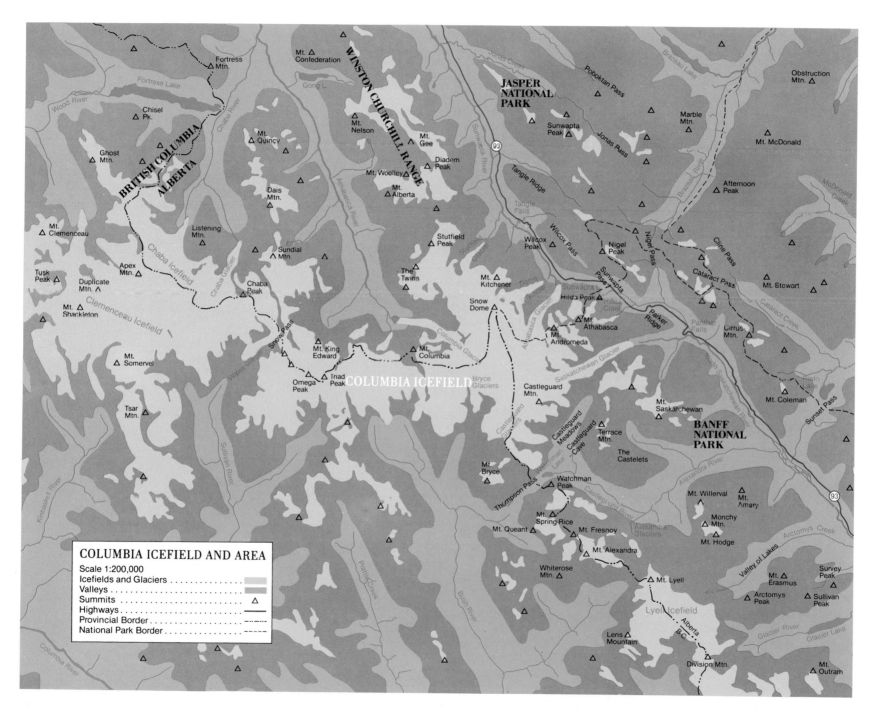

COLUMBIA ICEFIELD AND AREA

Scale 1:200,000
Icefields and Glaciers . . . .
Valleys . . . .
Summits . . . . △
Highways . . . .
Provincial Border . . . .
National Park Border . . . .

JASPER NATIONAL PARK

BANFF NATIONAL PARK

WINSTON CHURCHILL RANGE

BRITISH COLUMBIA
ALBERTA

COLUMBIA ICEFIELD

Fortress Mtn.
Mt. Confederation
Chisel Pk.
Ghost Mtn.
Mt. Quincy
Mt. Nelson
Mt. Gee
Diadem Peak
Mt. Woolley
Mt. Alberta
Dais Mtn.
Mt. Clemenceau
Listening Mtn.
Sundial Mtn.
Stutfield Peak
Tusk Peak
Apex Mtn.
Duplicate Mtn.
Chaba Peak
The Twins
Mt. Kitchener
Snow Dome
Hilda Peak
Mt. Athabasca
Mt. Andromeda
Mt. Shackleton
Mt. Somervel
Snow Pass
Mt. King Edward
Mt. Columbia
Bryce Glaciers
Castleguard Mtn.
Omega Peak
Triad Peak
Tsar Mtn.
Mt. Saskatchewan
Castleguard Meadows
Castleguard Cave
Terrace Mtn.
The Castelets
Mt. Bryce
Watchman Peak
Mt. Spring-Rice
Mt. Queant
Mt. Fresnoy
Mt. Alexandra
Whiterose Mtn.
Mt. Willerval
Mt. Amery
Monchy Mtn.
Mt. Hodge
Mt. Lyell
Mt. Erasmus
Arctomys Peak
Survey Peak
Sullivan Peak
Lens Mountain
Lyell Icefield
Alberta B.C.
Division Mtn.
Mt. Outram

Poboktan Pass
Sunwapta Peak
Jonas Pass
Marble Mtn.
Obstruction Mtn.
Mt. McDonald
Afternoon Peak
Tangle Ridge
Tangle Falls
Wilcox Peak
Wilcox Pass
Nigel Peak
Nigel Pass
Cline Pass
Cataract Pass
Mt. Stewart
Sunwapta Pass
Parker Ridge
Hilda Creek
Panther Falls
Cirrus Mtn.
Mt. Coleman
Sunset Pass

Fortress Lake
Wood River
Gong L.
Jonas Creek
Brazeau Lake
Sunwapta River
Chaba River
Athabasca River
Chaba Icefield
Chaba Glacier
Clemenceau Icefield
Columbia Glacier
Athabasca Glacier
Saskatchewan Glacier
North Saskatchewan River
Plato Lake
McDonald Creek
Brazeau River
Dome Glacier
Stutfield Glacier
Kimbasket River
Sullivan River
Wales Glacier
Castleguard Glaciers
Watchman Lake
Thompson Pass
Castleguard River
Alexandra River
Alexandra Glaciers
Valley of Lakes
Arctomys Creek
Bush River
Pratt Creek
Columbia River
Glacier River
Glacier Lake

93

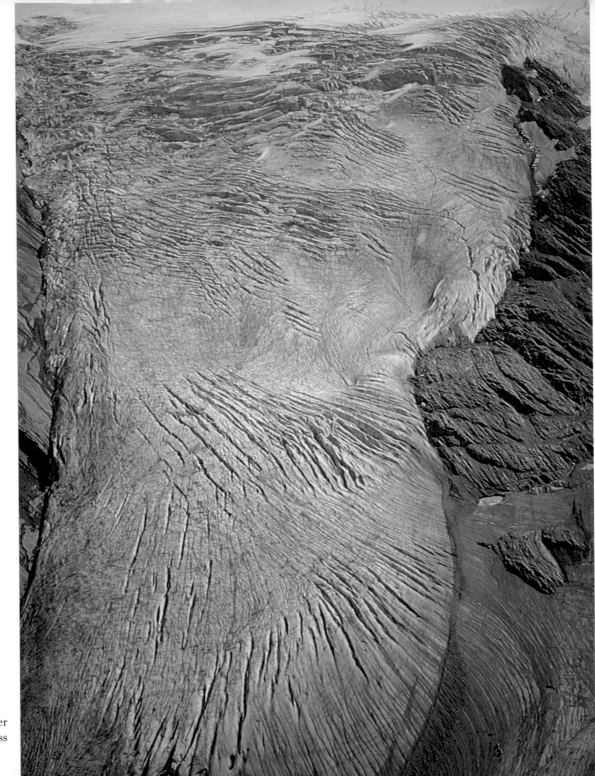

Unnamed glacier
near Snow Pass

Randkluft,
Mount Andromeda

Icefalls, Athabasca Glacier,
Mount Andromeda
icefall in foreground

Meltwater stream, Athabasca Glacier

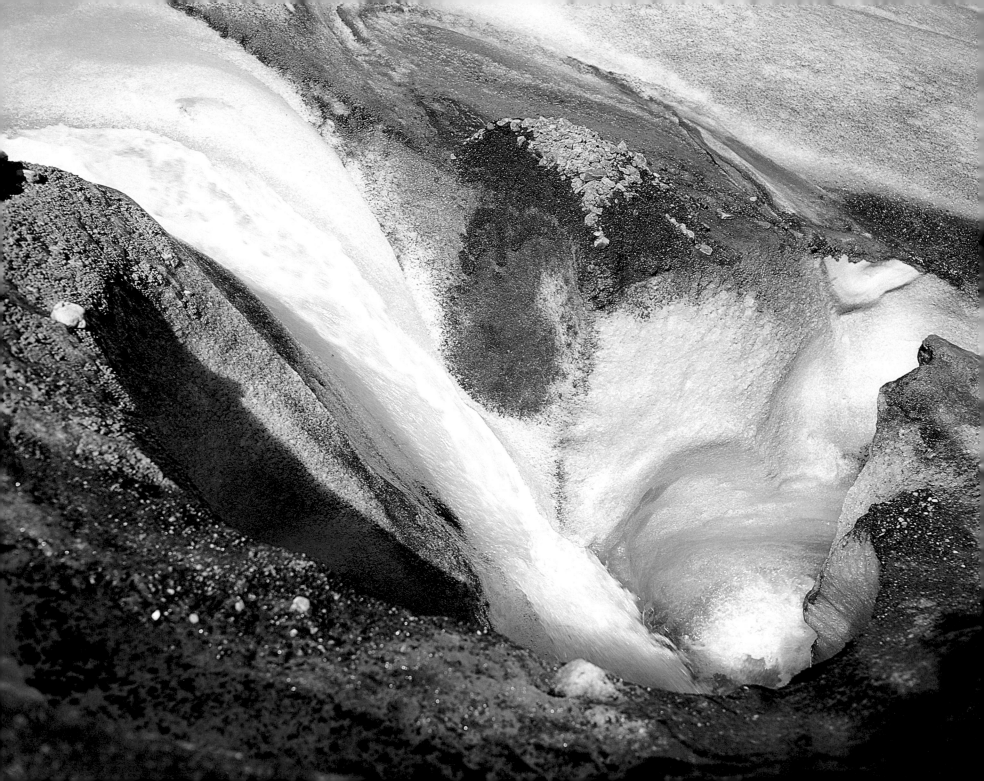

The amount of water running in any glacial stream fluctuates dramatically both with time of day and season. Volume is minimal during the winter, when new snow mantles the entire glacier, and maximal during the late summer months. Diurnally, the flow is greatest in the late afternoon, after the sun has put in a full day's work on the glacier face. A party ascending a glacier in early morning steps easily over small rivulets that become raging torrents by five in the afternoon.

Glacier silt

Meltwater, typically arrayed in an extensive system of dendritic tributaries, can flow long distances over a glacier. Very few streams, however, run their entire course on top of the ice. Most eventually plunge into cracks and crevasses worn quickly into exquisitely-sculpted and finely-polished blue punctures termed *moulins* or *mill holes,* so named because the water spiralling into them sounds like an old-time water mill. The stream boils into the moulin, crashes against the opposing wall, and begins a swirling descent into the bowels of the ice. A large moulin may be several metres across, its sides often scalloped, fluted, and undercut, bearing witness to the water's changing course as it weathers away the cavity.

Impressive as they are, few moulins penetrate the full depth of thick glaciers, and the meltwater continues downglacier via fissures and tunnels within the ice itself. Such *englacial streams* eventually reappear at the margins or toe of the glacier, exiting from beautifully-carved *ice caves,* the mouths of which can be sizeable caverns. In recent years the toe of Athabasca Glacier has sported a cave entrance between ten and fifteen metres wide, equally high, and close to thirty metres deep.

Moraines. Glaciers transport more than ice and water. Rock rubble, weathered away from the surrounding mountains, continually tumbles onto a glacier's margins. The ice acquires debris by its own action as well: glaciers constantly scour their stoney channels, plucking rock from their beds and walls. Like a heavy-duty conveyor belt, the ice carries its load down the valley to deposit it below, sorting it and shaping it as it moves. The deposits are called *moraines,* and there are several types, each classified according to location, form, and composition.

One of the more conspicuous is the *lateral moraine,* a sharp-edged ridge of breccia delineating the margins of a valley glacier's ablation zone. Rock falling onto the glacier sides insulates the ice

beneath, protecting it from the full force of the summer sun. The central portion of a glacier undergoes extensive melting (or *down wasting*) as it descends into the valley, but the ice along the borders, insulated by the rock, maintains a higher profile and can become a pronounced feature. Lateral moraines become particularly obvious if the glacier supporting them begins to retreat (and most mountain glaciers have been retreating for the past hundred years): the abandoned moraines mark the line of the glacier's greatest advance. These moraines can be very steep and contain a core of ice. The surface rock is often quite loose, poised just at the angle of repose, making for difficult, if not downright treacherous, hiking. And, as the redoubtable Mark Twain observed, ''a moraine is an ugly thing to assault head first.''

When two streams of ice, each with its burden of debris, coalesce to share a single valley outlet, *medial moraines* form. The rubble of the adjoining edges–rubble which would normally form lateral moraines for two separate glaciers–jumble together to create a strand of stone and mud snaking down the central portion of the newly-constituted glacier. The greater the number of ice streams joining together, the greater the number of medial moraines.

Several kinds of moraines delineate a glacier's toe; collectively they are known as *end moraines*. One such type common to the glaciers of the Columbia Icefield is the *recessional moraine*. Once a glacier begins to retreat, it drops the debris it carted downvalley at the toe of the glacier. The ice simply melts out from under its load of rock. If the retreat should stall, and the glacier toe remain stationary for a year or two (the degree of melting temporarily balanced by the downvalley flow of ice), the debris deposited at the toe can form a substantial ridge–a recessional moraine. Another type of end moraine, one which delimits the furthest advance of a glacier, is a *terminal moraine*.

Lateral moraine, Athabasca Glacier; Mount Andromeda behind

24

Morainal till, Stutfield Glacier terminus

BEYOND THE MOUNTAIN WALL

The whole country is verry Rough
and the weather in July will freeze a kyote
so I am sure you would call it Grand.

Fred Stephens, letter to Walter Wilcox

II

BEYOND THE MOUNTAIN WALL

A UGUST, EARLY MORNING. Deep cobalt sky: cool, clear air, sweet enough to drink. In good voice, a Brewer's Sparrow sings a waking song in a low copse of willow nearby. Below, a boisterous mountain freshet wends its way toward a rising sun. From its gravel pad, nose down, the helicopter eases up, yaws left a degree or two, corrects, then rises quickly. In seconds we are out of the valley shadows. Dark spruce fall away and bright sun breaks across our plexiglass bubble. The steady vibration of the blades slicing air and the sudden warmth of the sun lull me; my ears pop; a finger taps my shoulder.

"The light meter," Don shouts. "I forgot it. We'll have to turn around." He is crouched in the back, a small arsenal of photographic equipment beside him on the seat.

I begin to relay the message to our pilot, Jim Davies, but he's already heard it and is initiating the turn. Jim, a quiet man, contemplative and forgiving, shows no sign of distress at lost time and fuel.

"Wait a minute!" A cry of triumph. "Here it is." Jim smiles, shakes his head slightly, and completes the turn, now 360 degreees. "These photographers," he muses into the headset, "are all alike."

This morning we're flying from Bow Summit and our objective is the Columbia Icefield. We're attempting a counterclockwise tour, a weaving circumnavigation of peaks and glaciers: up Saskatchewan Glacier, hang a right to follow the ice over the heads of Athabasca, Dome, Kitchener and Stutfield Glaciers, circle the Twins, shoot past the toe of Columbia Glacier and lose ourselves, as usual, in the vicinity of Snow Pass, where the Columbia merges with the Chaba and Clemenceau Icefields. From Snow Pass it's back along the southern margins of the ice, past Omega and Triad Peaks, and the Bryce and Castleguard Glaciers, to complete the loop.

Helicopters aren't my favourite means of transportation. They offer little of the sensual experience associated with more traditional modes of mountain travel–walking, skiing, horseback riding, canoeing, and dog-sledding–but they are terrific overview machines. Two hours in a helicopter and one can see more of the mountains than he could in a summer of hiking, and can collate bits and pieces of topography that defy assemblage when experienced at ground level. And a collation is what we're seeking today. After five summers of probing valleys and climbing ridges on foot, we're ready to put the whole thing together. It's not our first flight, but we hope it will be the one finally to pull sense out of a ramshackle corner of God's good household.

Flying north-northwest from Bow Summit, we follow first the Mistaya River and then the North Saskatchewan. The rivers, vigorous and rolling, glint from serpentine, braided courses. Brilliant turquoise lakes–Peyto, Mistaya, Waterfowl, and Glacier–flash in the sun as we sweep by above. Glaciers flare from the ragged peaks on our left: we are approaching the soul of the Main Ranges of the Canadian Rocky Mountains.

Glaciers, or the ghosts of glaciers, are everywhere here. And well they should be–four times since the advent of the Pleistocene Era (roughly a million years ago) ice has overwhelmed these mountains, plucking, scouring, scrubbing, scratching, polishing, rasping, tearing, spindling, and mutilating them. The amount of damage is unimaginable. Consider: the meltwater streams flowing into Sunwapta Lake at the toe of Athabasca Glacier deposit 570 tonnes of torn down shale, dolomite, limestone, sandstone, and quartzite on a good summer day. Five hundred and seventy tonnes of rock, sand, clay, and silt a day carried into one small lake at the foot of one (relatively) small valley glacier. How can we begin to think about the debris from glacier sheets large enough to swallow the entire mountain range, overriding the minor peaks completely and surging well up the slopes of the very highest? Geomorphologists estimate that the major

ice advances removed ten metres of rock from five and a quarter million square kilometres of land.

The last big advance of the Pleistocene, the Wisconsin,* which sheathed the Rockies in ice up to a kilometre deep, retreated from the major valleys less than 10,000 years ago, and left reluctant vestiges of the once omnipresent ice among the loftiest, most desolate peaks. Thus we find the Columbia Icefield and the other tattered remnants of ice crowning the crest of the continent. Not that the ice has been complacent since the Wisconsin began to subside; lesser advances and retreats have continued unabated through the centuries. The last surge culminated in the mid 1800's, neatly overlapping the European exploration of the Rockies. Scarcely a hundred years ago, the Columbia Icefield was a third again larger than it is today.

Glacier ghosts? The valleys, overdeepened and widened by repeated glacier assaults, all exhibit a characteristic "U" shape**; tributary valleys, once filled with ice flowing to join the major glacier arteries, now "hang," suspended hundreds of metres above the valley floor; braided rivers and streams run a maze of different beds, cutting new ones as glacial-quarried and transported rubble rapidly fills in the old ones; lakes form behind old moraines and lie trapped in glacier *cirques****; rocks are variously gouged or polished, bearing the scars of having been dragged along the bottom of moving ice or of having rocks dragged across them. The ice of millenia has opened

*Three distinct local glacial surges associated with the Wisconsin affected the Icefield: the Bow Valley Advance (dated at 25,000 to 20,000 years Before Present), the Canmore Advance (18,000 to 12,000 B.P.), and the Eisenhower Junction Advance (12,000 to 9,930 B.P.). Of these the Canmore Advance was the greatest, flooding the valleys with a network of ice 450 to 800 metres thick and reaching an altitude of 2440 metres above sea level.

**A stream-eroded valley normally exhibits a "V" shaped cross-section; a glacier moving down such a valley deepens and widens it to a broad "U".

***A *cirque* is a glacier-carved bowl, often of great dimension, formed as a glacier scours a nest for itself in the mountain uplands. Typically, a glacier forms in a high rock niche or water-eroded pocket and, as years pass, picks away at the surrounding rock until it has eaten a considerable cavity in the mountainside. In times of warmer weather the glacier melts, leaving a handsome basin for a lake in its stead. A glacier still occupying such a spot is a *cirque glacier*.

up the mountains, keeping them youthful in appearance even while carrying them off to three oceans.

As we near Mount Saskatchewan, Jim opens the Bell's throttle and we soar up and across the peak's eastern flank to pick up the Saskatchewan tongue. Nine kilometres long and over a kilometre and a half wide at its annual snowline, the Saskatchewan is the single largest outlet of the Columbia Icefield, but it receives only a fraction of the attention lavished on its sister tongue, the Athabasca. A low rise of bedrock which resisted the Saskatchewan's advances of the mid-1850's is just large enough to hide the glacier from the Icefields Parkway, the popular highway stretching from Lake Louise, in Banff National Park, to Jasper townsite, in Jasper National Park. The Athabasca tongue, however, descending from the Icefield just a few kilometres to the northwest, encountered no bedrock to hinder or hide it, and pushed just far enough to choke off the valley before beginning its retreat. Eighty years later, in the 1930's, the construction crews of the Parkway blithely skirted the morainal rubble of what is today the most easily accessible glacier in North America.

This morning the Saskatchewan tongue lies broad and blank below us, thoroughly tamed by an ameliorating climate. Since its big push of the 1800's, the glacier has retreated twelve hundred metres and has down-wasted nearly thirty, despite a centreline ice velocity of seventy-five metres per year. Its path of withdrawal is marked by a valley bottom plain of rock detritus ranging from two and three-metre boulders to particles of sand and silt, but it consists mostly of rounded rocks the size of a human head or slightly smaller, just right for twisting ankles. Called *ground moraine,* the rubble dropped from the retreating ice. A brown, muddy sluice of water, choked with sediment, braids itself down the plain, headed for Hudson Bay.

The Saskatchewan's snout is severely flattened, a function of both glacier decay and a smooth glacier bed. Probably no other Icefield outlet is so easy to climb. One short step from morainal flats to ice and one is on his way up the glacier. In summer the glacier face is an uneasy topography of minor humps and slumps and hissing meltwater; in winter it is a gently rising ramp of wind-swept snow. It is nowhere seriously crevassed, but a series of marginal fissures dominates its southern reaches and demands some navigational expertise should one wander onto that section of the glacier.

Opposite the crevasses, running down the northern border of the glacier, is a well-developed medial moraine, one of the best examples the Icefield has to offer. Originating near the glacier's snowline, where a tributary glacier marches down from the southwest peak of Mount Andromeda, the moraine runs the entire length of the tongue.

The tributary responsible for the moraine, six hundred vertical metres of tumbling, ruinous ice, now lies to our right; Castleguard Mountain is on our left. Jim reins our mechanical Pegasus to the north and suddenly we're out over the Icefield proper. Sunlight slithers across the great rolling expanse of snow and ice below, catching on the swells, shooting across the troughs to ricochet off sheer mountain cathedral walls. It is, at 230 square kilometres, a splendid and disturbing configuration of rock, snow, and ice–the largest icefield in the Rocky Mountains.

It is North America ten and twenty thousand years ago: harsh, elemental, threatening. We can imagine–and find in ourselves–the fears of the first Americans, the nomadic Siberian hunters, who crossed the Bering land bridge more than 10,000 years ago* to make their way south through passages between the retreating continental sheets. Here are desolation and wildness and mystery to summon

*Geologists believe conditions would have favoured such migrations between twenty and forty thousand years ago, and again between twelve and thirteen thousand years ago.

30

ancient terrors from the hidden recesses of the soul. And beauty enough to allay them.

The helicopter is flying at just under 3350 metres, not even as high as the circumglacial summits and only 450 metres above the average altitude of the ice below. From our vantage the Icefield is a snowbound plain of little relief, yet sensuous in the relief it exhibits, gently rising and falling, rolling in vast undulations across its mountain cradle. The mountains themselves are transfigured. The ice-encircling peaks–the single greatest collection of mountains over 3200 metres in the Canadian Rockies–which from the outer valley bottoms soar in precipitous leaps of greys, blues, browns, and pale yellows, within the perimeter of the snowy bastion are soft and flowing contours of white and pale blue. It is a surprising contrast: a gentle, albeit grandiose, hummock of snow rising 700 to 750 metres from the Icefield abruptly drops away to the valley floor beyond in a stark escarpment of 1000 to 1500 metres. For the mountaineer working from within the Icefield margins, Snow Dome, Mount Kitchener, Stutfield Peak, North Twin, South Twin, Mount Columbia, Mount King Edward, and Castleguard Mountain are all little more than very long, tiring, moderate-angle snow trudges.*

The Icefield is as irregular in form as it is regular in relief. If we could triple our helicopter's altitude, we would see something much less intimate and considerably more bizarre. From 9000 metres or more the Icefield is an enormous bluish-white freak alpine amoeba, corpulent pseudopodia pulsing out in all directions to engulf a barren limestone prey. The main body of the Icefield has two main axes, giving it the appearance of a slightly skewed and very ragged Latin cross. One axis runs due west, stretching from the terminus of the Saskatchewan tongue to the unnamed peaks flanking Snow Pass at

the western extremities of the Icefield, nearly thirty kilometres distant. The other axis runs northwest from Castleguard Mountain and the Castleguard Glaciers to Stutfield Peak, a span of over eighteen kilometres.

Despite its proximity to a major road–meaning easy access to naturalists of all persuasions–many of the answers to questions concerning the Columbia Icefield have been slow to emerge. Not until 1979 did cartographers scientifically delimit the size of the Icefield (with disastrous results: the once advertised "largest icefield in North America" lost nearly a hundred square kilometres from its previously estimated area of 325 square kilometres), and only in the last years of the seventies have glaciologists made progress measuring the depth of the Icefield. The depth studies, by no means conclusive or comprehensive, have established a range from a minimum of around a hundred metres to a maximum of 365 metres. This statistic has been a bit disappointing as well: it represents a drop in estimated thickness of nearly six hundred metres.

The precise number of glaciers the Columbia Icefield nourishes remains unknown. No inventory has been made to date, but approximately thirty glaciers are fed by the Icefield. The most accessible glaciers have been catalogued, officially named, and examined with varying degrees of thoroughness–the Castleguard, Saskatchewan, Athabasca, Dome, and Columbia Glaciers, along with their tributaries and a few major outlets terminating in the vicinity of the Icefields Parkway–but others, equally impressive, lie along the remote western and southwestern marches of the Icefield. Early explorers and mountaineers named some of these unsung glaciers, but such appellations (Horseshoe, Ontario, Manitoba, Toronto) have withered from lack of use and the ice awaits rediscovery and naming anew.

The person who claims "if you've seen one glacier, you've seen them all," has obviously only seen one glacier and not paid much

---

*Information pertaining to elevations and first ascents, etc., is in Appendix 1, page 102.

attention to it at that. Different settings, contours, features, and degrees of activity combine to give each glacier its own distinctive personality. A few, like the Saskatchewan, are basically complacent and easy-going; some, like Columbia, are savagely intemperate; others, like Athabasca, are more vain than tempestuous–natural entertainers; and yet others, like Pranghorn, are intimate, almost confiding in nature. For the person who spends substantial time clambering around them, exploring their nooks and crannies, they become like family, and one seeks them out depending on his mood.

From the top of the Saskatchewan tongue we set a course for Snow Dome, a little more than eight kilometres to the northwest. Within minutes we are flying over the catchment area of Athabasca Glacier and Don requests a slow turn over the region: he has spotted some spectacular crevasses off the southeast flank of Snow Dome, marking the juncture of the ice flowing off the Dome and the ice moving down the Athabasca tongue. We circle in low for a better look and find the crevasses enormous, gaping blue mouths each large enough to swallow a fleet of Winnebagos.

On our second swing past the crevasses we shoot out over the topmost of the three icefalls gracing Athabasca Glacier. It is not as large a glacier as Saskatchewan, but it is more picturesque, a fortunate attribute since it is photographed by thousands of people each year.

It has also been the object of more scientific research than any of the other Icefield outlets. Tourists visiting the Park's Information Bureau, The Icefields Centre, across the valley from the glacier toe, or riding one of the snowmobiles a short distance up the tongue, quickly learn the vital statistics: 5.3 kilometres long, a little over a kilometre wide, 304 metres maximum depth just below the lower icefall. The glacier descends, like the Saskatchewan, close to six hundred vertical metres from snowline to terminus at Sunwapta Lake,

and its *response time*–the time it takes any given portion of ice to move from snowline to snout–is 150 years. In keeping with the historical pattern of the Icefield, the Athabasca tongue advanced significantly in both the eighteenth and nineteenth centuries. Since the 1850's it has retreated nearly 1 520 metres and in recent decades has averaged a recession of just over twelve metres a year. Or, as one zealous scientist determined, 5.1 millimetres per hour–at the base of the terminus during the summer months.

Millimetres aside, Athabasca Glacier has a number of distinctive features which contribute to its reputation as a showpiece. A textbook example of a lateral moraine rises from its eastern flank, soaring 124 metres above the valley floor. Its core of ice, a remnant of the advance of the 1850's, serves as an armature for a knife-edged ridge that leaves an impressive outline of what the glacier was like a little more than a hundred years ago.

The glacier also boasts a beautiful ice cavern, carved by a melt-water stream issuing from the northwest corner of the snout. Since wastage constantly alters the terminus of the glacier, an ice cave is bound to be ephemeral, but the Athabasca toe has consistently displayed a major grotto since people first began to visit the glacier.

Any ice cave is imposing; a large one can be something from a dream. Where else could one expect to stumble into a dark blue room with walls and ceiling of faceted ice as sleek and slick as polished glass? In some spots the ice is plane-smooth; in others its surface becomes a random grouping of shallow concave lenses ten centimetres to a metre in diameter. Some of the ice is so clear one can see into it for decimetres and not be quite sure at what depth darkness prevails; some is punctuated with delicate white feathers of entombed air trailing off into successively deeper shades of blue; some is seamed and broken and blocks of transparent ice alternate with blocks of milky, white-blue frozen bubbles. Streaks of sunlight filter back from the cavern entrance, coruscating off burnished edges, and the sound of moving water echoes eerily out of cold, dark niches.

A fitting oracle; a place of dreams, enchantments, visions. And of peril. During the autumn of 1978 a slab of ice several metres thick and twice as long spalled from the domed roof of the Athabasca cave and nearly crushed a good-sized handful of Parks Canada naturalists. Their exit was both unanimous and hasty.

As the naturalists knew when they entered the cave, glacier exploration involves risk. It is simply impossible to predict the precise moment of an ice cave's collapse, or the toppling of a twenty-metre high serac, or the failure of a snow bridge spanning a great crevasse. And yet, as most mountaineers will readily attest, it is just such "fine-print" unpredictability which accounts for part of the attraction of glacier travel. The little bubble of uncertainty, the slight touch of the unknown, keeps the soul from turning stale.

In the spring of 1978, while attempting to photograph a large mill hole, Don, Edward Cavell (another photographer), and I ran afoul of an electrical hail storm. Storms brew up in the mountains almost instantaneously, as if conjured out of blue sky by evil magic; by the time we realized an outbreak was imminent we were already immersed. A glacier, we were to learn, is no place to weather an electrical storm: a lightning strike skitters long distances across a glacier's face, posing a serious threat to anyone on the ice.

As we abandoned the photography and started looking for a quick way off the ice, the world exploded into a bright and glowing orange ball. One moment I was walking soddenly downglacier, wet hailstones peppering my back, and the next it seemed I was slowly awakening in a wonderfully comfortable bed on a warm spring morning with a peculiar orange light flooding the room. I discovered, though, as I tried to rise from the bed to investigate the light, that I had misplaced my legs, and without them had little hope of finding them. Fortunately, full feeling returned with full consciousness. Ignoring the fact my toes seemed to have been blown off (I noticed my boots, at least, were still intact), I turned to Don, still sprawled on the ice a few metres behind me, who agreed we should be on our way. He promised to join me as soon as he found his own legs. Edward, barely visible through the blowing mists, having seen us alive, was already in full sprint. We were approximately a kilometre from the margins of the ice, and our dash for safety emphatically pressed home a lesson we of twentieth century North America have largely forgotten: man, alone and in the face of indifferent nature, is an absurdly frail, timorous creature. If none of us would care to relive those minutes on the ice, neither would any of us disavow the wisdom they imparted.

Today, in flight, cocooned in the seeming security of our air-flailing technology, we sweep quickly past Snow Dome where we spot two very small, moving specks of colour on the mountain's southern flank at about the 3040 metre mark. Two stalwart spirits, no doubt learning some lessons of their own, are struggling toward the summit, two climbers magnificently dwarfed by their environment. Snow Dome is, in fact, a singularly unimpressive ascent but it is not without allurements. From its summit there is an unimpeded view of what is generally regarded as the scenic culmination of 650 unbroken kilometres of mountains, a goal worthy in itself, and one stands, at 52° 12′ north latitude, 117° 19′ west longitude, on the hydrographic apex of the continent, the only point in North America from which water flows to three oceans. The Columbia Icefield in general, and Snow Dome in particular, is the major tri-partite divide in North America. Spill a cup of tea on the summit of Snow Dome, the old tale goes, and its molecules will eventually reach the Pacific, Atlantic, and Arctic Oceans.

The Icefield writes large the same story. Meltwater from the

Castleguard and Saskatchewan Glaciers and the southeast quadrant of the Icefield flows to the North Saskatchewan River and thence to Lake Winnipeg and Hudson Bay via the Nelson River. From the outlets of the Icefield's northern spur, including Athabasca, Dome, Columbia, and several unnamed glaciers beyond Mounts Columbia and King Edward, issue the headwaters of the Athabasca River, a tributary of the Mackenzie River which flows to the Beaufort Sea. From the remote western reaches of the Icefield, where numerous unnamed glaciers feed the Bush and Sullivan Rivers, comes substantial nourishment for the Columbia River, draining into the Pacific Ocean many kilometres to the southwest. It makes kicking over one's Thermos almost worthwhile.

Beyond Snow Dome we make a tight swing around the head of Dome Glacier, slip by Mount Kitchener on the west, cut across the double icefall of Stutfield Glacier and finally arc back to the south, circling the northern guardians of the Icefield: Stutfield Peak and the Twins.

The tongues of the glaciers of Snow Dome, Mount Kitchener, and Stutfield Peak are the poor cousins of Athabasca and Saskatchewan Glaciers, but they deserve at least brief mention. From the helicopter it can be seen that the glaciers tumble off a highly convoluted but continuous 910-metre wall running from Athabasca to Stutfield Peak. One can imagine a monolithic block of rock out of which the ice of ages has slowly chiseled a series of great cirques, each cirque embracing its own glacier. Where the wall doesn't have a glacier pouring over it, it lies blanketed by a layer of pale green-blue ice a hundred metres thick, an imposing sight from the valley bottom and the Icefields Parkway.

The glaciers are undernourished compared to Athabasca and Saskatchewan and are much smaller, but they do feature stately icefalls of 750 metres and more. In this regard the Kitchener Glacier is unique in that it is a *regenerated* glacier, one composed of ice which has actually free-fallen from the rim of the Icefield above and reconstituted itself on the valley floor. The Stutfield Glacier, equally impressive, features two distinct icefalls which merge in the valley to form one glacier tongue.

Much of the ice constituting the Dome, Kitchener, and Stutfield tongues is covered with a rock mantle up to a metre thick. A portion of the rubble comes from falling rock, weathered from the deeply-eroded mountain walls cradling the glaciers, and the rest is carried by the ice itself as it grinds its way down the precipitous mountain face. The rock carried within the ice is exposed as the ice melts in the warm valley below and is termed *ablation moraine.** Over thirty-five percent of the Dome Glacier tongue has such a covering, and over sixty percent of the Kitchener and Stutfield tongues are similarly insulated.

South of the South Twin we encounter a tremendous amphitheatre dominated by Mount Columbia and Columbia Glacier. From the head of Saskatchewan Glacier, Mount Columbia appeared a gently rising ramp of snow and ice; now, turned ninety degrees, it is a gnarled, precipitous black pyramid of shattered stone, shot with belts of treacherous ice and rising nearly 1525 vertical metres from its base. From the top of Mount Columbia to the Athabasca River valley bottom there is a vertical difference of 2308.5 metres, the maximum relief found in the Icefield environs.

The north face of Mount Columbia, viewed from the valley floor, demands respect, if not devotion. Don has dedicated a portion of his life to the photographic worship of the mountain, but his dedication to date has been ill-rewarded. One lengthy pack trip up the Athabasca River was cut short by a surly outfitter who realized his horses

*Ablation moraine, in disctinction from ground moraine (page 30), rests on ice; once the ice melts away completely it becomes ground moraine.

would have a tough time surviving on spruce boughs and limestone; heavy rains and a grizzly looking for a little variety in *his* diet thwarted another effort. Smoke, low clouds, and bad light have all hallmarked our previous airborne expeditions. Today, early as we are, the sun is careening around the amphitheatre in a thin, bright way that bodes no good.

Columbia glacier at least is in full light, regardless of the light's quality. A classic glacier. From over 2736 metres on the Icefield proper it begins a slow roll into the valley, picking up momentum as it moves over an increasingly sheer bedrock cliff. At 1975 metres it abruptly levels out and begins a long, stately procession toward a small meltwater lake a little more than seven and a half kilometres distant. It is a thin, tapering, elegant glacier, and exhibits a striking series of *ogives*,* alternating bands of dark and white ice extending in a gently arcing pattern across the glacier tongue.

Columbia Glacier is the only glacier emanating from the Icefield which terminates in a lake (the Athabasca tongue ends a short distance above Sunwapta Lake), and small icebergs, or *growlers*, continually calve off the toe of the glacier to create small fleets of intricately sculpted ships. The combination of the iceberged lake, the long curving arc of glacier, and Mount Columbia rising above the icefall creates a singular, spectacular scene.

There is little time to savour the view, however. The sun is getting high, the light more difficult, and we want to spend any extra minutes we might have today at the far western end of the Icefield.

After a quick pass over Columbia Glacier we head due west, skirting the Icefield to the north, passing Mount King Edward (with a rock face nearly as impressive as Columbia's), to enter another amphitheatre of rock and ice. As Columbia Glacier constitutes the west branch of the headwaters of the Athabasca River, so the unnamed glaciers surrounding us now constitute the east branch.

Flying directly toward the Great Divide we rapidly approach the western limit, the Hall of the Mountain King, a place of few people and forgotten names. A low, broad, glaciated passage offers itself just to the south and we take it, slipping into British Columbia. Jim points the helicopter toward a prominent outcrop, and just below Snow Pass, just beyond the Columbia Icefield, we settle down for lunch at the edge of the world.

*The formation of ogives is directly related to the seasonal movement of ice down a steep, narrow icefall. During the summer months, when the ice is moving rapidly, it is badly stretched and torn, and accumulates a variety of rock debris, dirt, dust, and blowing pollen.
A degree of melting and refreezing occurs, meaning an enlargement of ice crystals. At the bottom of the icefall the broken ice is compressed, resulting in dark blue, bubble-free, dirt-discoloured ice. The ice passing through the icefall during the winter, however, moves more slowly–entailing less fracturing during the fall and less compression at the bottom of the fall–and is protected from debris by a thick blanket of snow. This "winter" ice emerges on the glacier tongue as light, bubbly bands of milky-white ice, alternating with the darker bands of "summer ice."

Saskatchewan Glacier

Crevasses, Snow Dome

Athabasca Glacier   Crevasse interior

Athabasca Glacier terminus

40

The northeast margin of the Columbia Icefield; looking across Mount Stutfield and Stutfield Glacier to Mount Kitchener (left) and Snow Dome, Mounts Athabasca and Andromeda on far horizon

Looking west across the summit of Stutfield Peak to Mount Alberta; North Twin on left

Mount Columbia and Mt. King Edward from the north

Columbia Glacier

Columbia Glacier; North Twin on right

Ah, yes. The edge of the world. Crumbling rock, spilling ice, a few million cubic kilometres of blue sky pushing all the way to the Pacific, and a few patches of orange-gold lichen at our feet. A breath of air, fresh and cold enough to beckon tears to the eye. Trickling waters so clear and delicious one could believe them nutritious. On sun-warmed boulders we eat lunch and enjoy the crescendo of the mountain range. To the west stretches the Clemenceau Icefield, unmeasured but mapped as large as the Columbia; to the north, adjoining the Clemenceau, smaller but of similar timbre, lies the Chaba Icefield; to the east runs the spidery pointer of the Columbia.

There is a jump in scale here. Unnamed mountains, known to climbers only by their altitudes (Peak 10,096, and so on), soar a thousand metres and more above our already dizzying perch while sinisterly shadowed and precipitous canyons carve down a thousand metres or more. Objects in our peripheral vision twitch and jump. Dropped here by helicopter today—no time for us to acclimatize gradually—we feel we might have stumbled out into a bright, hot afternoon from an extended mid-day session in a dark, quiet tavern.

We wander to the brink of our limestone outcrop to inspect the Wales Glacier, a shattered, nightmarish finger more crevasse than ice. To cross here, would be impossible. Insbustantial fins of ice and excesses of what a climber calls terminal air do not a walkway make.

From Snow Pass we fly first south and then due west, the anonymous summits and glaciers of the Icefield's southernmost margins glistening under the high sun. Don shoots rapid-fire with his Leica, hoping to record the entire length of ice. Our earlier sojourns followed more haphazard routes, photography was more selective, and our ensuing attempts to put together a cohesive overview from the resulting images were comedies of argument. Too much ice, too much rock, too many angles, too many mysteries abound in this undisturbed land. Undisturbed and, seemingly, unwanted. For Parks Canada the southwest reaches of the Icefield don't exist; for British Columbia the underlying rock has proven of little mineral–and thus financial–importance. For the casual tourist the region is unthinkably remote and inaccessible. Someone once said wilderness is a function of the distance from the nearest road and the altitude above it. I would add the nature of the intervening terrain. Here we are at neither a great remove from the nearest road, nor a great distance above it, but the character of those horizontal and vertical metres insures its wild status. To the north, east, and west, the ice itself is protection; to the south, the wild gorges and chaotic forests of the Sullivan and Bush River drainages are no man's land. A spirited letter from a turn-of-the-century outfitter, Fred Stephens, to an American client, Walter Wilcox, describes the quintessential ecstasy of travel in the B.C. bush:

> ...i will just give you a Pointer to Pass it by...never saw sutch undergrowth, mud and wet, with mosquitoes that would stop a syclone, the poor Englishmen[Stephens' clients]looked like Plum Puddings walking around with their faces swoolen up to twice their Natural size...It was raining 7 days out of 6, to make it more Pleasant. The Pack horses got covered with Brittish Columbia mold, the oat meal soured, the hard tack swelled up... The wood would not burn and a few more things went Rong. We finally got up the River far enough so it commenced to get deep and the valley was Narrow and filled with Burnt fallen timber... We found it impossible to follow up the valley to the foot of Mt. Bryce and Columbia so we took to the hills and camped 7000 above sea Level. Here it snowed for 4 days and the wind blowed so we had to tie down the Pack Saddles to keep them in camp. I suppose this would be Delightful to you But somehow it don't catch me...

There is little to report on this remote stretch, except that it is a pristine solitude. In a distance of over twenty-five kilometres only two names, Omega Peak and Triad Peak, appear on the map. Uncounted tongues of ice sprawl and slip from the high plain, spawning bright freshets and rivers which fall away to the Pacific. A few climbers, a few geographers, a few goats, and the odd grizzly know the area, but otherwise it is unmeasured, unprobed, inviolate.

The high, triple-peaked summit of Mount Bryce slides by on our right as we once again cross the Great Divide, trading British Columbia for Alberta. Below lie the several arms of the Castleguard Glaciers, the southernmost extremities of the Icefield. We swing north again, traversing the length of the Castleguard Meadows to reach Saskatchewan Glacier and complete our circumnavigation.

The meadows below, however, detain us, and we circle them slowly, recalling our fine days of hiking, skiing, and riding there. Occupying a shallow trough carved by the glaciers of past millennia (carbon-dated layers of ash found in the soil of the meadows show the most recent glaciation occurred before 9,600 years ago), the meadows measure approximately five and a half kilometres long by one and a half wide, and constitute a unique environment in Banff National Park. Aesthetically they are a delight, a high alpine oasis in a wasteland of ice and stone: geologically a fascination.

Rain and meltwater containing carbon dioxide readily dissolve limestone, dolomite, and gypsum: where this happens on a large scale—as in the Castleguard Meadows—a *karst topography* is generated, characterized by various types of sinkholes, caves, and elaborate drainage systems. For thousands of years both rain and meltwater have been eating away at the formations of limestone underlying the meadows, turning the layers of rock into a honeycomb of drainage tunnels. The system feeds a series of springs which discharge hundreds of metres below the elevation of the meadow's surface into the Castleguard River.

Surface karst phenomena include *flutes,* shallow furrows etched in exposed rock. Water streaming down flutes, and more deeply-etched *rills,* seeps into fissures in the rock and dissolves it to depths of ten metres or more, creating *karst hollows.* Large funnel-shaped depressions known as *ponors* pockmark the meadows. Up to several metres in diameter, ponors indicate karst hollows forming below the soil: as the hollows grow in size overlying soil slumps into them.

The most interesting Karst feature associated with the meadows, though, is a cave—longest, and one of the deepest and oldest, in Canada. From its entrance just below the southern lip of the Castleguard Meadows (at 1980 metres above sea level), Castleguard Cave gradually ascends to the northwest, penetrating the core of Castleguard Mountain and running on for several kilometres beneath the ponderous bulk of the Columbia Icefield. From its entrance to its uppermost passages the cave rises nearly 300 metres, and because it runs further beneath existing glaciers than any other known cave it has earned an international reputation. Speleologists and cavers rank it, in terms of uniqueness, with the Mammoth Cave–Flint Ridge system in Kentucky, the Gouffre de la Pierre St. Martin in France, and the Carlsbad Caverns in New Mexico.

Over the past fifteen years geologists have spent thousands of manhours exploring and charting nearly eighteen kilometres of passageways. Although exploration has yet to discover any major western exit (promising leads have ended in ice-plugged shafts and boulder-choked chambers), it has led to an equally exciting discovery: the probable existence of a cave of equal or larger dimension running far beneath Castleguard Cave. It is believed the new, lower cave, named Castleguard II, now carries a large underground river which once flowed, more than 350,000 years ago, through the upper, relic cave. It is, like so many things here, a mystery. May it long so remain.*

*A brief discussion of the cave's discovery and exploration is found on page 80.

48

Ghastly, and scarred, and riven. — Is this the scene
Where the old Earthquake-demon taught her young
Ruin? Where these their toys? or did a sea
Of fire envelop once this silent snow?
None can reply — all seems eternal now.

Shelley, *Mont Blanc*

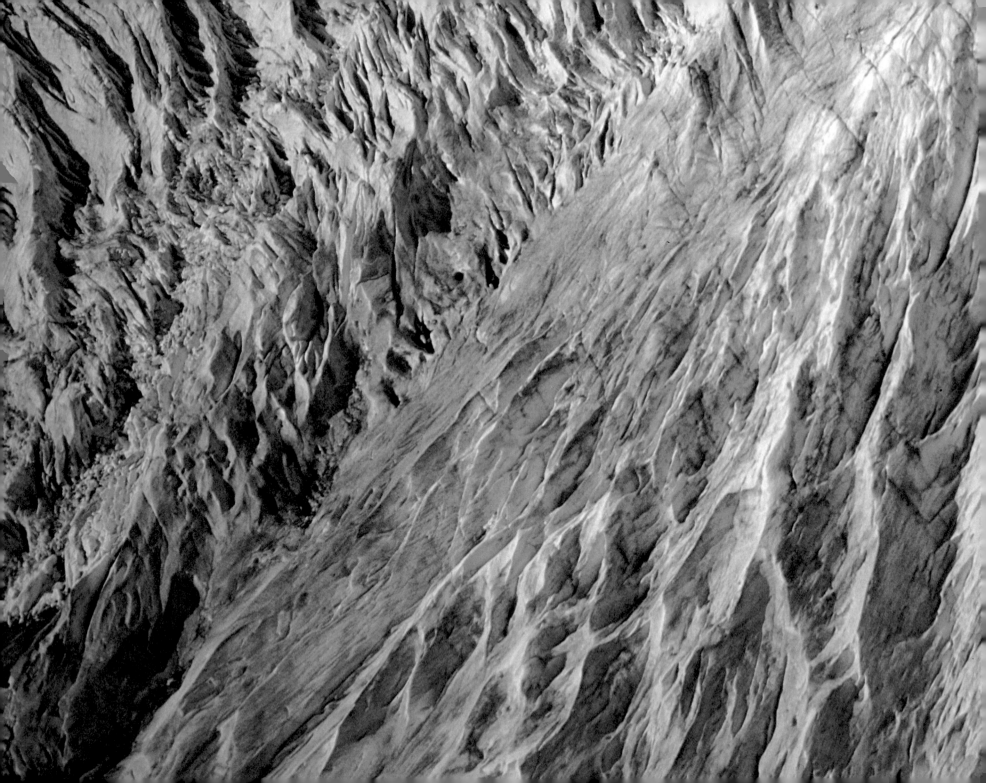

Wales Glacier   Omega Peak

Headwaters
of the Bush River
below Mount Bryce

Bryce Glacier

North Castleguard Glacier;
the Twins in the distance

Watchman Peak
above the Castleguard
River

Castleguard Cave

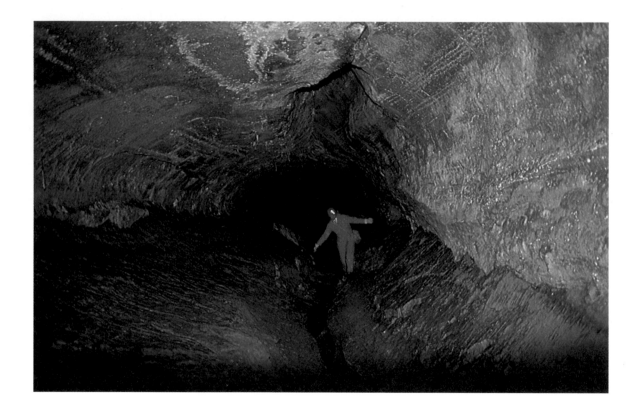

Caver in Castleguard Cave

Castleguard Meadows;
Watchman Peak behind

Castleguard River

A
DANCE WITH
WHITE DRAGONS

The Discovery and Exploration of the Columbia Icefield

Those were glorious days for the explorer - the "Great
Lone Land" was waiting for the first footsteps; there was
the fascination of the unknown; one never knew what the
morrow might bring forth; there was:
"Something hidden. Go and find it. Go and look behind the Ranges -
Something lost behind the Ranges. Lost and waiting for you. Go!"

J. Norman Collie (quoting Rudyard Kipling)

III

A DANCE WITH WHITE DRAGONS

THE HUMAN HISTORY of the Canadian Rockies shimmers with the lives of hardy, resilient, resourceful, competent, and independent characters: flamboyant, one-of-a-kind, never-before never-again personalities who found in the mountains lives to match their exceptional energies and unusual sensibilities.

The explanation of the disproportionately high number of sinewy people lies in the mountains themselves. A harsh climate denies much: strong winds favour high spirits; cold rains and cruel flinders demand wilful souls. Only the most robust of any species—plant, animal, human—thrives at altitude. There is also a particular truth to be found at treeline—a finely-attuned and exaggerated sense of being, a harmonized sense of self and world—which, once felt, makes dropping like a rock into the gaping maw of a crevasse more desirable than tumbling heartsick back to the anonymity of large cities and the monotony of flatland.

Some will argue the proposition. The Indians first travelling the Rockies—the Stoneys, Kootenays, Crees, Interior Salish, and Plains Blackfoot—found little to sustain either body or soul, and nearly all the first fur traders and explorers, once finished their mountain sojourns, retreated quickly to Montreal's comforts. They were seeking trade rather than mystery, profit rather than grandeur, but even then some remained in the wilderness, or returned at first opportunity.

Their recounted stories stirred others to see firsthand the hinterland described in fashions to stretch the limits of civilized credulity. Two fabulous mountains stood high in the imagination: awesome, spearhead snags of stone and glacier, the highest of the entire continent. With Circean appeal, rumour of the peaks attracted adventurers, scientists, and alpinists to the Rockies; and the explorations of such men led to the discovery of the Columbia Icefield. The tale of the two mountains gives shape and texture to the subsequent exploration of the Icefield itself...

Mount Bryce from the summit of Mount Castleguard, 1924

David Thompson, a man whom many historians consider North America's premier geographer and mapmaker, was, in January, 1811, the first European to cross Athabasca Pass and one of the few to visit the Rockies.* Thompson's employer, the North West Company–a fur trading company determined to dominate the business at the expense of its rival, the Hudson's Bay Company–had decided as early as the mid-1780's to extend its domain to the Pacific coast, and Thompson was one of the men it sent west to find a feasible route through the mountains.

Probing the valleys of the major rivers flowing east from the mountains, Thompson in 1807 had located Howse Pass, a low, broad gap easing through the Rockies fifty kilometres southeast of the Columbia Icefield. Peigan Indians, upset by the murder of one of their fellows by a member of the Lewis and Clark Expedition, blocked the route, and by the late autumn of 1810 Thomson was seeking a more northerly route to the Pacific. Tracing the reaches of the Athabasca River, he began his ascent of Athabasca Pass in the first days of January, 1811. "My men were the most hardy that could be picked out of a hundred brave hardy men," he later wrote, "but the scene of desolation before us was dreadful, and I knew it." Encouraging his men, who were fearful that "the haunt of the mammoth is about this defile," and struggling against temperatures as low as minus twenty-six degrees Fahrenheit, Thompson reached "the height of land" on the tenth of the month. Eighty kilometres northwest of the Icefield, Athabasca Pass was not so convenient a route as Howse Pass, but it was traversable and the Nor'Westers made good use of it throughout the second decade of the nineteenth century. The Main Ranges between Howse Pass and Athabasca Pass remained unexplored.

Thompson's scientific observations were usually accurate, but he wildly miscalculated Athabasca Pass' altitude. Using a traditional method to determine elevation, measuring the boiling point of water, he reckoned the pass at 11,000 feet (3353 metres), somewhat more than twice its actual altitude. He then estimated that the flanking mountains rose another 7,000 feet (2133 metres) above the pass, another error, though not so serious as the first.*

If, in fact, the summits guarding Athabasca Pass weren't so high as Thompson's calculated elevation of the pass itself, they seemed quite high enough to early travellers. The chidden landscape, the hardships endured to reach the pass, and the intimidating countenance of the bastions rearing above it conspired to support their exalted height. Ross Cox, another Nor'Wester who crossed the pass in 1817, recorded the effect it had on his party:

> One of our rough-spun, unsophisticated Canadians, after gazing upwards for some time in silent wonder, exclaimed with much vehemence, 'I'll take my oath, my dear friends, that God Almighty never made such a place!'

It was a Scots botanist, David Douglas, who popularized the notion of two prodigious peaks. Crossing the pass from west to east in the spring of 1827 with a Hudson's Bay fur brigade, Douglas spent five hours one afternoon climbing a mountain just west of the pass (a task involving labours "great beyond description") and later declared it to be "the highest yet known in North America." He named the peak Mount Brown, honouring his patron, a famous British botanist of the day. Another summit, rising on the far side of the pass, he christened Mount Hooker, in recognition of W.J. Hooker, one of Douglas'

---

*This is the generally accepted story. There is, however, a good deal of controversy surrounding Thompson's error. In one draft of his memoirs, written forty years after he completed his mountain wanderings, he implies he made the calculations himself; in another draft he quotes Sir George Simpson, who didn't cross the pass until 1841, as the source for the 11,000 foot figure. In fact, except for Thompson's reputation (which is not to be taken lightly, certainly), it makes little difference to the ensuing story, for other men following Thompson made their own estimations, and almost without exception they gave credence to the exaggerated altitude of the pass.

*Fur trader Anthony Henday had been the first to see the "Shining Mountains" in 1754.

former professors, later the Director of the Royal Botanical Gardens at Kew.

Was Douglas guilty of "enhancing" the story of his crossing once back in England and writing up his field notes for public presentation? In his original journals, he makes no reference to the altitudes of the mountains and, indeed, writes that from the summit of Mount Brown he could see nothing but "Mountains such as I was on, and many higher..." Furthermore, once he had decided Mount Brown was the highest peak in North America, his subsequent presentations reported varying altitudes and locations for the mountains. The public, perhaps blinded by the grandeur of the description, failed to note his discrepancies.

The two mountains made their official debut on a map published in 1829 that Douglas supervised: Brown lying west of Athabasca Pass at a denoted elevation of 16,000 feet (4877 metres), Hooker to the east at 15,700 feet (4572 metres). Douglas died shortly after the publication of the map (his eyesight failing, he stumbled into a bullock pit in Hawaii and was gored to death by a wild bull). His mountains prospered, appearing in atlases and on globes detailing the wonders of western Canada.

No sooner had the mountains been mapped, however, when the major route through the Rockies changed, this time to Yellowhead Pass, further north and considered to be faster and less arduous. Athabasca Pass fell into disuse, and although those few who made the traverse and kept journals–including a painter, a priest, and two British spies–made note of the spectacular scenery, none of them mentioned mountains of exceptional height. Mounts Brown and Hooker, charted but unobserved, awaited another generation of men, with other motives, to come searching.

It wasn't until 1884 that a tall, bespectacled, and articulate mountain wanderer and geology professor from Toronto, A.P. Cole-man, decided to travel west to find the two great summits. "A high mountain," he later wrote, "is always a seduction, but a mountain with a mystery is doubly so...I studied the atlas and saw Mounts Brown and Hooker...(and) I longed to visit them."

Coleman's decision marked the beginning of a new era of exploration and discovery, one which was to see detailed mapping of the major features of the Main Ranges of the Rockies, including the Columbia Icefield. It heralded a new way of looking at mountains, for the men and women who dominated the new era came not to exploit the fur-bearing resources of the mountains but simply to explore and enjoy an untrampled wilderness.

The new attitude reflected a change in European aesthetic and scientific values. When Douglas climbed Mount Brown (and thus became the first person to scale a continental divide peak–evidently no one had experienced any need or desire to do so before) and found "the view from the summit...too awful to afford pleasure," he was voicing a traditional European viewpoint. Travellers in the Alps in the Middle Ages wore blindfolds, convinced that the sight of mountains, like seeing the Medusa, would cause insanity. Master John de Bremble, a medieval monk, wrote, upon crossing the Col du Grand Saint-Bernard: "Lord, restore me to my brethren, that I may tell them that they come not to this place of torment." The scholar Vadianus scaled "the very high mountain" Pilatus in 1518, and returned to confirm the fact that Pilate appeared every Good Friday at the summit lake to receive counsel from Satan. Even the demure hills of England could evoke a negative response: Charles Cotton's addendum to Izaak Walton's *Compleat Angler* relates the comments of a London man who journeyed into the hill country: "I'll no more on thee; I'll go twenty miles about first. Puh. I sweat, that my shirt sticks to my back." No insanity, but a degree of discomfort.

It wasn't until well into the 1700's that people began to view

A.P. Coleman in Wilcox Pass, 1907

mountains as anything other than satanic deformations of the sweet earth's visage. The intellectual and cultural awakenings of the Renaissance broke the fearful vision of the medieval world, and the scientific explosion of the following centuries wrought great changes in the way men viewed themselves and the world in which they lived. It was inevitable that someone would discover mountains. When it happened, it happened in a big way. Naturalists hied themselves unto the hills simply to see what they might find and discovered to their delight that mountains were actually agents not of insanity but inspiration.

The discovery fortuitously coincided with the birth of Romanticism (it's difficult to tell which came first, each seemed to nourish the other), and the likes of Shelley, Byron, Wordsworth, and Goethe, exalting nature over artifice and energy over restraint, spread the good word quickly.

The British became particularly enamoured of the mountain world, and it is interesting to note–by way of explaining the almost overnight popularity of mountains–that many of the first alpinists came from two very different groups: the clergy and the scientists. The clergymen, according to mountaineering historian Ronald Clark, came to the mountains at a time when religion "had become a matter more of cross-referencing than of basic faith," and found in mountains a reaffirmation of belief and "a link between themselves and the unexplained and the inexplicable."

The scientists–many of them geologists–needed as well to "get beyond the slick certainties of life to the point where doubts arose." In their case, Clark believes,

> …it was not so much a question of religious belief as an intellectual problem posed by expanding knowledge which was the difficulty; yet with them also, the climbing of difficult mountains restored the balance. The academic as well as the physical and spiritual problems

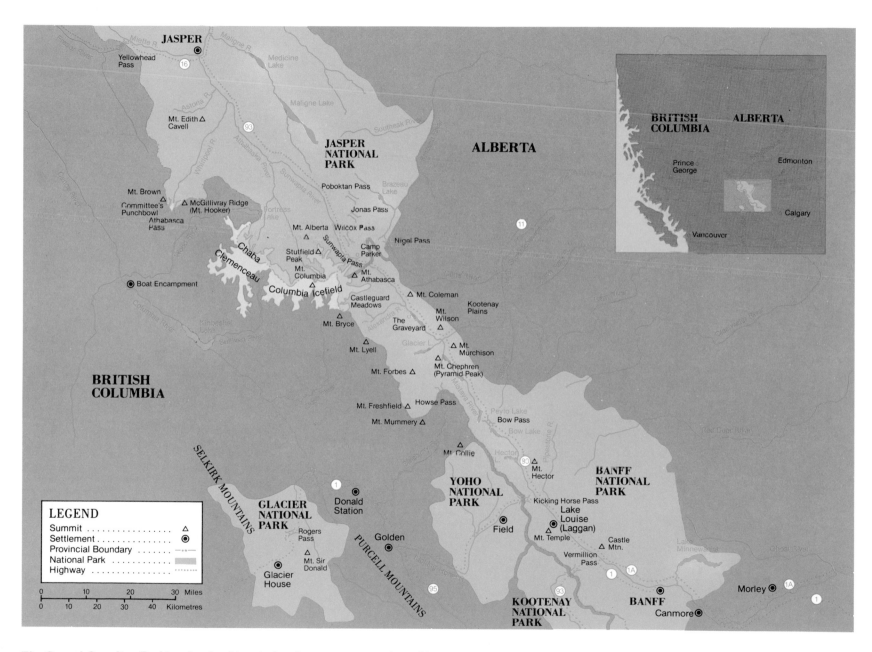

The Central Canadian Rockies showing historical and contemporary points of interest

they found gave them back their necessary unknown and made them complete men once again... They realised that to regain something that their age had lost they had to give genuine hostage to fortune; they had, at some period in the process, really to stand alone and be battered by the gale with only a fair chance of getting home alive. Nothing less would do.*

Mountains represented mystery, eternal values of form and beauty, romance, high adventure, and scientific endeavour; they thus befitted perfectly the energy, enthusiasm, and imagination of the Victorian Age. After seven unsuccessful attempts, the British artist Edward Whymper attained the summit of the Matterhorn in 1865, and within five years every major European peak had been climbed.

The Alps "conquered," alpinists looked elsewhere for new and untrodden summits. What targets more obvious than the two highest mountains of North America? The completion of the Canadian Pacific Railroad in 1886 meant easy access to the Rockies, and the bustling little resort of Banff provided a solid base for outfitting expeditions into the "great lone land."**

Reaching the Rockies was easy: locating Mounts Brown and Hooker was a problem of considerable magnitude. The immensity of the mountain range, indeterminate weather, and the bewilderments of navigating through muskeg and shintangle in largely uncharted country led to one confusing failure after another. Literature and maps were scarce to nonexistent, the old trails overgrown.

It wasn't, in fact, until his fifth trip to the western mountains that Professor Coleman found what he sought. During his first two

trips, in 1884 and 1885, he was content to ride the CPR to track's end (Laggan, or Lake Louise, in 1884, and on into the Selkirk Mountains–a range just west of the Rockies–in 1885) and then strike out on foot, horse, or canoe to explore whatever caught his fancy. At one point during the 1885 outing, he found himself at the Big Bend of the Columbia River, a well-known landmark to the voyageur of earlier days, and joyously realized that to reach the two titans "all one had to do was to canoe seventy miles down the Columbia (from the railroad) and then follow the old portage trail up Wood River...to the foot of Mount Hooker."

Easily said. In July, 1888, Coleman and a young companion, Frank Stover, "who had never paddled a canoe, nor climbed a mountain, nor shot a grizzly, and earnestly desired to do these things," embarked on what they later referred to as "our fiasco on the Columbia." Battling bugs, brush, and white water, the men were bitten, bruised, beaten, and drenched. "Every yard meant a struggle and every stumble meant a handful of prickles from the devil's clubs. It was mournfully enlightening to Frank." They couldn't chop their way through the heavy bush and they couldn't paddle their way down the heavy water. Frank became ill; provisions dwindled. With dogged determination they forged on for eleven days, expecting at every step to stumble across the old fur trade trail. Finally, down to three days' supply of food, they admitted defeat.

Failure only whetted Coleman's appetite. In 1892 he returned to the Rockies, "all the more eager to come to close quarters with the giants." Accompanied by his brother and three other acquaintances, plus two Stoney Indian Guides, Coleman set out again, this time on horseback, and travelling north-west through the foothills, where "there was trouble in muskegs and fallen timber, and everyone was disillusioned and disgusted and wondered why he had come into a world of so much tribulation and such poor scenery," the party

*Clark, Ronald. *The Victorian Mountaineers.* London: B.T. Batsford Ltd., 1953. For other sources on the changing attitudes of men toward mountains see the "Mountain Metaphysics" section of the suggested reading list at the end of the book.

**A combination of natural hot springs, a Valkyrian setting, and unbridled CPR promotion gave Banff an international status almost before the completion of the railroad. By the late 1880's the town was rife with outfitters, packers, and alpine guides, the latter especially imported from Europe by the Railway for its clientele's convenience.

entered the mountains via the Brazeau River, cut across Poboktan Pass to the Sunwapta River, and then followed the Athabasca and Chaba Rivers as far as Fortress Lake. The Whirlpool River and Athabasca Pass, unfortunately, lay one drainage further north.

Realizing they had missed their mark, the men climbed a peak above Fortress Lake and looked in vain for mountains rising thousands of feet above the summits of the immediate vicinity, which Coleman determined to be only of the ten and eleven thousand foot variety. That night, Coleman later recalled, "we were cross as we lit a fire and made supper, and all sorts of doubts troubled us as to our position."

Perseverance, it is said, furthers, and Coleman, returning once again in 1893, at last located Athabasca Pass and the two elusive mountains. It was a catastrophe. Nine years' expectations and, in one quick glimpse, the professor understood the mountains "were a fraud." His measurements showed Mount Brown to be just over 9,000 feet (2743 metres) and Mount Hooker (today McGillivray Ridge) to be just under. "What," he indignantly wondered, "had gone wrong with these two might peaks that they should shrink seven thousand feet in altitude? and how could anyone, even a botanist like Douglas, make so monumental a blunder?" It was a crushing blow.

Coleman's journeys, though, were not without reward. He had, found Hooker and Brown; he had become intimate with large tracts of mountain wilderness previously unknown; and he became the first person to see the Columbia Icefield, even if he failed to recognize its true extent or nature. In 1892, from a mountain top near the forks of the Brazeau River, Coleman and a companion saw, in the distance (about twenty kilometres to the southwest), "splendid snowfields and peaks and walls of cliff." The region looked promisingly severe, and the men hoped it might be the abode of Brown and Hooker.

The reception given Coleman's exposé of the fraudulent peaks must have been as great a disappointment as the mountains themselves. Legends don't die easily, and other would-be explorers and alpinists, still wishing to believe in the monumental mountains, thought the blundering might be Coleman's. Perhaps, some nay-sayers suggested, the good professor had found the wrong pass. Anything, after all, was possible in that most confusing labryinth of peaks.

One such sceptic was Walter D. Wilcox, an American alpinist from Washington, D.C., who pioneered many important climbs in both the Rocky and Selkirk Mountains. Hearing Coleman's conclusions on Mounts Brown and Hooker, he decided "the subject seemed worthy of further investigation," and in 1896 organized a sixty-day expedition "for the purpose of visiting and measuring the mountains." From an historical perspective, his journey's importance lay more in the approach than the findings: rather than seek Brown and Hooker from the east or west, as Coleman had, Wilcox opted for a southern approach. Working up the Bow River from Lake Louise, he crossed Bow Pass to the Mistaya and North Saskatchewan Rivers, traversed Wilcox Pass to the Sunwapta River, and then proceeded down the Sunwapta to its confluence with the Athabasca River, a distance of approximately 230 kilometres. It was to become a standard route for expeditions exploring the Main Ranges.

With two local packers, Fred Stephens and Tom Lusk, and a cook, Arthur Arnold, Wilcox and a fellow mountaineer, R.L. Barrett, started north from Lake Louise on July twelfth.* The trip was an eventful one, filled with hard work, discovery, and yet more mysteries. Life on the trail was as exciting as arduous. "We were," Wilcox

---

*Nearly all expeditions into the Rockies were outfitted in Banff and generally consisted of one or two wealthy clients, two or three packers, a cook, and often one or more alpine guides. Much of the rich anecdotal history of the Rockies revolves around the colourful exploits of the guides and packers. Coleman, whose brother ran a ranch near Morley (half way between Banff and Calgary), had local access to horses and supplies and organized his journeys independently.

later recounted, "surrounded by muskegs, burnt timber, and bad language."

One of the party's greatest obstacles was the unfamiliarity of the country: "We could get no information about the region, as no white man had been up there, and the Indians are very indefinite in geographical matters." To compound their route-finding perturbations, the men discovered "forest fires had consumed about one-quarter of all the timber land in the Canadian Rockies," and, as

anyone who has ever tried it can testify, cutting a trail through a burned-over lodgepole pine forest on a hot, muggy afternoon thick with mosquitoes, horseflies, blackflies, no-see-ums, and yellow-jackets is no picnic. Fording swollen, boulder-choked rivers resulted in perilous moments and wet larder. (It was standard practice for packers to allow the flour to be doused at the first crossing; the resulting crust of flour glue thereafter protected the core of usable material against inevitable abrasions, contusions, and subsequent soakings.)

And there were, of course, the horses. Excellent mountaineers the adventurers may have been; horsemen they were not. The packers had problems enough keeping the pack string in line; the clients, left to their own devices, rode the hard edge of disaster. It is conceivable the journals kept by those on the trail contain as much material concerning human/horse interaction as they do mountaineering. Coleman, some years before, had concluded that, "though filled with the spirit of the Evil One, horses could actually be induced to carry small loads in almost any direction..." J. Norman Collie, who was soon to follow Wilcox north, wrote: "There is a western saying to the effect that 'No man can serve God and drive oxen'; and a pack-team of cayooses can be equally relied on to evoke unchristian sentiments and purple patches of vituperation." And Wilcox and Barrett, only two days out of Lake Louise, learned an important and expensive lesson. Barrett, scouting a route through extensive muskeg,

> found a short cut across a narrow swamp, and said it was safe. Our horses followed, and before they had gone fifty yards, four of them were down in the bottomless swamp, with only their heads and ears alone visible.

What is safe for a man on foot, they quickly realized, is not always safe for horses. The animals were rescued, but only at the cost of half the outfit's sugar, all the baking soda, and most of the tea and coffee. It was a rather inauspicious beginning for a sixty-day journey.

71

After close to a month of toil and trial, sometimes making less than eight kilometres a day, the party neared the headwaters of the North Saskatchewan River. Exploring the various possibilities of a route into the next drainage system to the north–the Sunwapta River–Wilcox stumbled on both the Saskatchewan and Athabasca Glaciers. The Saskatchewan he viewed from a small mountain and described it as "a large, straight glacier...At least six or seven miles of this glacier is visible, and it may extend much farther behind the intervening mountains."

Athabasca's snout was discovered as the party moved across Sunwapta Pass and found the glacier tongue blocking any possible descent into the Sunwapta Valley. (In 1896 the glacier tongue still extended across the width of the valley.) The men were obliged to detour high and to the east of the glacier, traversing the pass now bearing Wilcox's name. From the rolling alpine meadows of the pass they saw "...a group of very high mountains. They were dome shaped and covered with immense snow fields..." There were also a series of cliffs "at the top of which there is an unbroken wall of glacier ice several miles in length in the form of a horseshoe." Wilcox, like Coleman before him, failed to realize the vast extent of the ice.

He did spot Mount Brown, although he failed to reach Athabasca Pass. His measurements of the peak tended to support Coleman's, but, confused by the location and height of Mount Hooker, he turned homeward, doubting even his own conclusions.

The ravelled threads of the lost mountain quest were next picked up by a quiet-spoken, often brooding Scots chemistry professor from the University of London. John Norman Collie, an alpinist of international repute, made his first excursion to the Rockies the year following Wilcox's riddle-filled sojourn. Climbing north of Bow Lake late in the season, Collie saw, fifty kilometres to the north, "a magnificent snow-covered mountain..., its west face falling sheer for thousands of feet." He estimated the peak to be "at least 15,000 feet high," a fact that immediately sparked his interest, for only two peaks of that size were marked on the map north of Mount Lyell. They were, of course, Brown and Hooker. Brown, he knew, had supposedly been dethroned, but the question of Mount Hooker was still open, and Coleman's interpretation of the peaks remained suspect.

The following summer Collie was back in the mountains, with two climbing companions, Herman Woolley and Hugh Stutfield. Bill Peyto, a legendary Rockies packer, met the three climbers at Laggan in late July and, accompanied by Peyto and his trail crew–Nigel Vavasour, Roy Douglas, and Bill Byers, the cook–the men started north, bound to settle the problem indisputably. The trip, reminiscent of Wilcox's, took nineteen days to reach Sunwapta Pass, and Collie's account has a familiar ring:

The next four days was one protracted struggle with woods, muskegs, horses, and our tempers; from early in the morning till late in the afternoon Peyto and the men chopped, and yet as a result of it all we only made about 10 miles...On the fourth day...Peyto returned about noon with the information that...this new valley was one mass of muskeg and water, and that no sane person would attempt to push on farther. This called for heroic measures, so I ignored Peyto's picturesque language and suggested whisky. This saved the situation...

The weather, at least, was respectable, if hot, and the climbing was superb. In later years Collie would also remember with fondness and humour the hours spent in camp at night, the men gathered around the fire:

Very tall were the yarns that circulated as the flames shot merrily upwards from the crackling logs, and the ruddy sparks flew aloft into the gloom to join company with the now dimly shining stars. Death, it was represented to us, confronted the backwoods traveller in quite a remarkable variety of shapes, and even if we did not break our necks

on the mountain, we gathered it would be hard times if some member of the outfit did not die of sunstroke, or drown when fording rivers. Finally, Woolley, remarking that it was getting late, announced that he was going to bed in his boots. This augmented Stutfield's already growing terror, for he slept with his head over Woolley's feet; and the latter, who was a noted footballer in his day, had a nasty way sometimes of practising place-kicks in his dreams.

Camping below Wilcox Pass on August 17, 1898, the men discovered their larder running low, and they realized their days on the trail that summer were numbered. Stutfield volunteered to hunt the following day, foregoing what promised to be an interesting climb on a peak just west of camp.

The ascent of that mountain, which they named Athabasca, was more difficult than they anticipated, and it wasn't until late in the day that Collie and Woolley reached the summit, at 3491 metres the highest yet attained in Canada. The rigourous climb was well worth the effort, for, as Collie later recalled:

> The view that lay before us in the evening light was one that does not often fall to the lot of modern mountaineers. A new world was spread at our feet: to the westward stretched a vast icefield probably never before seen by human eye, and surrounded by entirely unknown, unnamed, and unclimbed peaks.

He also recognized the mountain he had seen the year before:

> Chisel-shaped at the head, covered with glaciers and ice, it stood alone, and I at once recognized the great peak I was in search of; moreover, a short distance to the N.E. of this peak another, almost as high, also flat-topped, but ringed round with sheer black precipices, reared its head into the sky high above its fellows. At once I concluded these might be the two lost mountains...

Elated, the two men returned to camp to find Stutfield back from his hunt with three sheep, enough meat for several days. The men immediately decided to turn their attention to the Icefield.

Two nights later they camped high on the eastern margin of Athabasca Glacier and early the following morning began their bid for what Collie believed to be Mount Brown. His record of the attempt articulates a realization successive generations of Icefield climbers would echo: "...the peak we were walking towards was farther off than we imagined, for it lay on the opposite shore of this frozen ocean." After nine full hours of glacier hiking the men found themselves separated from the mountain by a vast amphitheatre of snow and ice, the summit itself still hours away. They retreated, but not before struggling up a "great dome of snow" rising over the eastern flank of the Icefield. This they named the Dome, today's Snow Dome.

The view from the Icefield convinced Collie and company the mountains seen were not Brown and Hooker but rather two new giants, which they christened Mount Columbia and Mount Alberta. Short of provisions again, the men made a quick foray into the environs north of the Icefield–which revealed no peaks comparable in size to their new discoveries–and then turned south toward Lake Louise. It was a hungry return: at one point their entire provender consisted of one sardine, two anchovies, and some dried meat, or "biltong," which Collie found "very sustaining but highly indigestible, and in appearance the reverse of appetizing." When Byers first tried to serve the meat, the men were convinced he "was serving the outfit with the uppers of Peyto's boots, which had recently shown signs of disintegration."

Back in England, Collie again turned his attention to Brown and Hooker, reading and rereading everything he could find on the matter. Unearthing a reference to one of Douglas' original journals, Collie noticed the botanist had scaled Mount Brown in a single afternoon. It was the missing piece to the puzzle:

Now it would have been quite impossible for Douglas to start at 1 in the afternoon, and get to the summit of either of the peaks that we thought might be Brown and Hooker [Columbia and Alberta]; in fact, it is highly improbable that he could have climbed them under any circumstances. That he ascended the peak that Professor Coleman's party climbed is much more probable, and to Professor Coleman belongs the credit of having settled with accuracy the real height of these mountains–namely, 9,000 feet.

It must have been with satisfaction that Collie penned an obituary for the myth of Brown and Hooker:

> For nearly seventy years they have been masquerading in every map as the highest peaks in the Canadian Rocky Mountains; they must now retire from that position, and Mts. Forbes, Columbia, Bryce, and Alberta will, in future, reign in their stead.

Although certain aspects of the Brown and Hooker question would return to haunt historians of a future generation,* the case, after seventy years, closed.

Collie introduced the Columbia Icefield to the world in an article published in the 1898 *Alpine Journal,* an introduction which greatly enhanced the growing reputation of the Canadian Rockies, and, in the years immediately following, inspired several expeditions intent on glacial exploration.

In 1900, a friend of Collie's, Charles S. Thompson, travelled up the Alexandra and Castleguard Rivers to the pass later named in Thompson's honour, hoping to meet Collie and Stutfield who were simultaneously battling their way up the Bush River from the west. Bad weather discouraged serious climbing on Thompson's part, and Collie's party failed even to reach the rendezvous.**

*See footnote, page 79.

**See letter, page 47.

The following summer a European explorer and professor of mathematics at the Sorbonne, Jean Habel, traversed Wilcox Pass (where he imagined himself "in High Asia, on a pass leading into Tibet") to investigate the headwaters of the Athabasca and Chaba Rivers. He felt his efforts achieved little,

> for, like all former expeditions, mine ran short of provisions, and we had to return a fortnight earlier than I expected, just when we had found the right way to advance on difficult ground, and in perfect weather...

But he nevertheless charted the northern reaches of the Icefield, passing directly beneath the towering north faces of Mount Alberta, North and South Twin, and Mount Columbia. (The northern and southern aspects of those mountains vary so greatly that Habel, failing to recognize them as the ones Collie described from the Icefield side, named them, respectively, La Pala, Alpha and Beta, and Gamma.)

Habel's journey was also, incidentally, responsible for a marvellous understatement concerning alpinism in the Icefield region. While climbing Mount Chaba, one of Habel's companions turned to him and said simply, "A man may break his neck here." Habel recalled, "I knew at once that we had attained the climax of our art."

In the summer of 1902, the Reverend James Outram, an energetic British alpinist who had taken up climbing as a cure for a general "brain collapse," decided to examine the area in which Thompson had had so little luck two years previously. Working with one of the CPR Swiss guides, Christian Kaufmann, Outram managed ten first ascents of peaks over 3050 metres and surveyed four new mountain passes during the course of a two month journey to the Icefield environs. Outfitted by Bill Peyto, the two climbers were accompanied by packers Jim Simpson and Fred Ballard.

The party lost little time in ascending the Bow and descending the Mistaya Rivers: previous expeditions had standardized the route and Jim and Fred had spent some time clearing trail of deadfall before Outram arrived in the Rockies. Less time fighting burnt timber meant more time on the mountains, and the two climbers of the party made good use of their mountaineering hours. Foremost among Outram's ascents was Mount Columbia. Camping near tree-line below the Castleguard Meadows on July 18 (where a campfire suddenly blazed out of control and nearly put an end to both the outfit and the forest of the upper Castleguard River), Outram's party was aware of the strenuous nature of the climb ahead, having heard from Collie of the problems to be expected on the Icefield. Accordingly, the climbers set out just before 2:30 a.m., proceeding up the South Castleguard Glacier to the Icefield proper and thence directly toward the mountain. It was a long haul, as expected, and Outram's account, partially detailed below, served well as a caution–and enticement–to those wishing to traverse the Icefield.

Progress up the Castleguard tongue in the half-light of dawn was slow, the snow and ice of the surface at times firm and relatively level, only to be dispersed by "a chaos of huge crevasses, wide chasms, and large, crater-like depressions seamed with smaller fissures...covered crevasses were numerous and some bridges called for the utmost of care." Gaining the Icefield plateau, Outram found

> the outlook fascinating in the extreme, though Mt. Columbia rose before us apparently as far away as ever.... Towards the north, above a sharp depression and beyond a magnificent cirque of rocks and glacier...were the Twins, the loftier pure white and its brother darkly impressive; then the immense area of snowfield sweeps upward to Mt. Douglas[now Mount Stutfield]and the Dome on the one side and dips to the green valleys of the West Branch Alexandra River and the Bush River on the other. Between these two rose the imposing walls of Mt. Bryce...whilst Mts. Athabasca and Saskatchewan stood guard over

the long, icy avenue to the head-waters of the North Fork of the Saskatchewan.

At 7:20, after five hours' work, the climbers stopped for breakfast, "well satisfied with our progress...but somewhat appalled at the way in which our peak appeared to retrograde as we approached, and at the growing softness of the snow." Sinking "deeper and deeper as the hot sun increased in power," the two lonely figures trudged on across the Icefield for another four hours. Reaching the bergschrund at the foot of the mountain at 11:30, Outram and Kaufmann left behind the equipment they felt they could do without and started up the broad eastern ramp of the mountain: "...we were soon engaged in pounding up a ladder-like arête [mountain ridge] of soft snow on a hard, slippery substratum, very likely under the scorching sun to avalanche. It was breathless work." Finally, at 2:30, twelve hours after they left camp, the men stood on the summit of Mount Columbia and, filled with the "thrill of exultation," rested for an hour on what they believed to be the "highest position in the Dominion of Canada."* The view from the summit was "simply marvellous":

> The vast extent of these mountain-top views is extremely striking, especially in such untrodden regions as the Canadian Rockies freely offer. The charm of the unknown is mingled with the pleasure of recognition. The climber knows not–no one living knows–what awaits him on the summit of a peak or pass. Bewildering hosts of splendid mountains, many unviewed by any one before; new valleys with their glaciers and foaming torrents, hitherto undreamt of tributaries of familiar rivers; the now revealed line of the erratic watershed, laid down by guesswork in the past,–these are some of the more fascinating revelations of the hour.

The descent was not quite so sublime. After plunging "gaily down

---

*It is, in fact, the second highest peak of the Rockies, surpassed by Mount Robson. Several higher mountains are found in the St. Elias Range in the Yukon.

the steep, soft slope" to where they'd left their excess gear, the men "embarked on the long journey over the interminable expanse of weary snow...At every step we sank in well above the ankles and usually to the knees, and, as we tramped monotonously onward, a sort of mirage formed upon the undulating surface of white snow."

The onset of evening tempered the heat of the sun and they hiked on through a golden sunset and into a full moon night. Dark belts of cloud, however, obscured the moon just as they reached the forest, and the men, safely off the glacier at last,

> entered the worst part of all the day's proceedings. To travel through a forest full of undergrowth and strewn with trunks of fallen trees is no easy task in broad daylight, but at night, without a moon, with limbs so tired that they would scarcely obey the order of the will, it was as tough a job as ever fell to our lot to undertake. Stumbling over stumps and stones, tumbling into holes and gullies, swinging across fallen logs, and fighting through the tangle bush, we dragged our weary way for two awful hours.

Shortly after midnight, twenty-two hours after setting out, the exhausted men dragged themselves into camp and roused the cook for a midnight supper.

Outram and Kaufman went on to climb Mount Bryce and Mount Lyell, both notable accomplishments, and then turned south to join forces with Collie and Stutfield for yet more first ascents. That Outram was first to reach Columbia's summit no doubt rankled Collie, who had become quite possessive of the Icefield. Earlier in the year he had written Thompson, referring to Outram as an "interloper" who should be prevented from reaping the rewards of others' labours.

Although Outram and Collie, *et al*, left dozens of mountains unscaled and many high passes unmapped, climbing expeditions to the Icefield tapered off significantly in the years between Outram's ascent of Mount Columbia and the end of World War One. There were, in fact, very few visits to the Icefield of any kind between 1902 and 1919, and few records of those are extant. Only Mary Schäffer, an intrepid Philadelphian, published an account of her Icefield visit. By including the Icefield on her itinerary of a summer's outing in 1907, Schäffer and her travelling companion Mary Adams earned the distinction of being the first white women to see the region. Prior to their trip it was taken for granted the long journey north from Lake Louise was simply too arduous for what in those days was still a fairer sex, but they ably put an end to such notions. After all, Schäffer argued, "We can starve as well as they; the muskeg will be no softer to sleep upon; the waters no deeper to swim, nor the bath colder if we fall in!" If, as is sometimes claimed, Schäffer was the first "real tourist" to view the Icefield – a claim propounded, no doubt, by mountaineers – she made a good job of it, exploring the margins of the ice from the north, at Mount Columbia; the east, from Wilcox Pass; and the south, at the foot of the Castleguard Glaciers.

The dozen years following Schäffer's grand tour were as quiet as the preceding five. Not until 1919, when a small crew of surveyors, members of the Alberta-British Columbia Interprovincial Boundary Commission, visited the environs, was a new contribution made to the slim volume of knowledge about the Icefield. A massive undertaking, the survey began in 1913 and involved eleven full summers of field work. Its goal was to delineate and map the Great Divide between the International Boundary and the point at which the divide intersects the 120th meridian of longitude – a distance of some eight hundred kilometres encompassing the wildest, most rugged portions of the Rockies.

The summer of 1919 was devoted to making sense of the sinuous watershed separating the two provinces in the vicinity of the Columbia Icefield, not an easy task. Based on an elaborate system of triangulation and phototopography (the use of photographs to pinpoint features and establish relationships between them), the survey was the first attempt to define the entirety of the Icefield topographically. It is a tribute to the crew's skill and determination that the information in the official reports is as accurate as it is; and it is indicative of the mountains' severity that the skilled and determined surveyors largely failed in their attempts to delimit the far western margins of the Icefield. Attempting to work down the Bush River, the men succeeded only in killing a horse, and despite their best efforts (including a first ascent of Mount Castleguard and a major excursion onto the Icefield to establish a series of survey stations), the Commission's map of the area confuses the sources of the Sullivan River.*

The work was significant. It pinpointed mountains and passes, indicated river drainages, named and described landforms (the Columbia Icefield was estimated to be 110 square miles in area, "discharging some twenty or more alpine glaciers, many presenting spectacularly beautiful waterfalls"), shot altitudes, and charted the Great Divide. The description of the latter is particularly interesting, for the men found that the watershed,

> having arrived at the summit of the Snow Dome…immediately turns back again upon its previous course and travels nearly due south over the icefield, slowly diverging westward, for a distance of three and a half miles, when it assumes a general course that is nearly due west.**

The surveyors were also the first to explore the Castleguard Mead-

---

*Working through Athabasca Pass, the Commission unwittingly stirred up the old Mounts Brown and Hooker debate. The surveyors, undecided as to which peak might be Mount Hooker, arbitrarily chose a mountain they felt fitted Douglas' description and christened it accordingly. The decision was contested by several climbers and historians and in 1928, on the occasion of the centenary of Douglas' ascent, J. Monroe Thorington, the premier climbing historian of the Rockies, published a paper in the *Canadian Alpine Journal* claiming that in fact McGillivray Ridge, a 3048-metre peak close by the pass, was the original Mount Hooker. A.O. Wheeler, a survey commissioner, defended the Commission's stance; Thorington defended his, and nothing was resolved. The facts, however, favour Thorington.

**Its peculiar course can be traced on the map on page 67.

---

ows, an "Arcadia for travellers owing to its bright sunny aspect"– an observation Don, and I disputed sixty years later as we sat through interminable days of intermittent rain and electrical storms.

During the course of the 1919 glacier chartings, the men of the Commission discovered more to survey than just mountains, for the Icefield, in the same summer, added yet another extraordinary woman to its list of visitors. Caroline Hinman, a capable and adventuresome sort from New Jersey, turned her passion for travel into a livelihood by organizing the first conducted trail rides in the Canadian Rockies. In 1919, after arranging successful camping trips in western Canada and the United States earlier in the decade, Hinman hired six guides and eighteen horses to escort herself and a retinue of fourteen young eastern women on a forty-day, 650-kilometre trip through the mountains as far as Nigel Pass and Athabasca Glacier. The trip was an unmitigated success and "Timberline Kate," as she became known to the packers, returned to the Rockies with her "Off the Beaten Track" tours almost annually until 1960. The Icefield was featured on many trips.

The 1920's saw a rekindling of mountaineering interest in the Columbia Icefield, and during the course of the decade the last of the Icefield peaks were subdued. Trails cut at the turn of the century became well-known and easy to traverse (what had been a three week thrash in the late nineties had become a comfortable five-day ride by the mid-twenties), and with each passing year more information on the Icefield became available.

Most climbing expeditions, after a pack trip to the Castleguard Meadows, established a base camp from which the alpinists would embark on long and arduous approaches to the outlying peaks. In late June and July, 1923, J. Monroe Thorington,* a prominent

---

*Thorington, one of the most literate and certainly the most historically conscious of the climbing pioneers, published *The Glittering Mountains of Canada* in 1925. It remains a classic "text" of Rockies mountaineering history today.

Philadelphia physician, along with W.S. Ladd and Canada's revered alpine guide, the Austrian Conrad Kain, established what they considered, "if there be any honour in it, a new long-distance and altitude record in Canadian mountaineering" by climbing, in five days, the North Twin (a first ascent and a hike of fifty-four kilometres); Mount Saskatchewan (first ascent, twenty-seven kilometres); and Mount Columbia (second ascent, forty-two kilometres). Thorington's tale of the North Twin climb is a familiar one: .

> It is a simple story: we saw our peak, walked toward it, up it, and back again. There was only the distance....The field is so huge. In one corner the stars were out; in another, beyond Mt. Athabasca, dark clouds hung and lightning flashed. We lit our lantern and went on through the night, pulling into camp at last, with morning light upon the hills as it had been twenty-three hours before when we departed.

At one point during the approach Thorington suffered from what he termed "fatigue mirages–momentary illusions–...; for an instant I was convinced that a dark line of distant crevasses was a staff planted on the summit...."

On their ascent of Mount Columbia the climbers were accompanied by their outfitter, Jimmy Simpson. Simpson, it will be recalled, had travelled with Outram on the occasion of the first ascent twenty-one years before, and it was a particular thrill for him to see what all the fuss had been about for all those years. He decided, upon reaching the summit, to climb Columbia every twenty-one years from then on. (Reminded of his resolution in 1944, Simpson said he'd undergone a change of heart: "Well, if I'd climbed it in 1902, that would be one thing, but since I didn't do it then, I can't see any reason to do it now.")

Simpson accomplished a "first" of his own on the 1923 expedition. Leaving the Castleguard Meadows, the party fulfilled Simpson's long-standing ambition to exit via Saskatchewan Glacier.

A perfectly logical exit, we might assume, until we remember the party included a string of twenty horses. Using the glacier's prominent medial moraine as a walkway, the horses, after some initial uneasiness, kept the situation well in hoof. On a trip of notable first ascents, it was a coup for the horseman to bag such a notable first descent. It was a route frequently taken in the following years.

Thorington's climb of twenty-three hours was not long for the record book. The following summer an expedition headed by another American climber, W.O. Field, undertook an ascent of both Twins (first ascent of the South, second of the North). The climbers left camp at 8:00 p.m., and hiked by moonlight to the base of the North Twin. Furious gusts of wind complicated their climbing, and Field later recalled that, "perched on a narrow ridge with appalling precipices on both sides, our insignificance in this particular part of the world was all too apparent." The return trip, like those of all previous expeditions, was an exercise in masochism. Wind, the burning intensity of light reflecting off the ice (so strong it can burn the inside of a climber's nostrils and even the roof of his mouth if he leaves it open), and fatigue all worked their sorcery:

> Mirages began to appear to us. Harris distinctly remembers bushes and trees growing at various places on the icefield, while I can with equal ease recall groups of people watching our pitilessly slow progress on that interminable march.

In just over twenty-four hours the men marched fifty-eight kilometres and reached two major summits.

Credit for the discovery of the Castleguard Cave also belongs to Field's party. Exploring the slope just below their camp in the Castleguard Meadows one afternoon, two of the men were startled by an ominous subterranean rumbling. Before they could consider what it might portend, a river burst forth from the side of mountain. Investigating, the men found the water to be flowing from a substantial

cave entrance. Two days later, after the water had subsided, the company penetrated the cave to a depth of some two hundred metres.

Later the same summer, another climbing team from the United States, Howard Palmer (a lawyer, businessman, and editor of the *American Alpine Journal*), and Dr. J.W.A. Hickson (a prominent philosophy professor and mountain metaphysician), spent three weeks with Conrad Kain exploring the region immediately north of the Icefield. Although bad weather forced the cancellation of most of their climbing plans (Mount Alberta was a high priority), the men did manage the first ascent of Mount King Edward. It was an especially gratifying achievement for Palmer, who had attempted the climb on a 1920 expedition to the headwaters of the Athabasca River and been turned back just two hundred metres short of the summit.

Field's endurance run of 1924, impressive though it was, was superseded in 1927 by the greatest of all Icefield marathons. A.J. Ostheimer, of the Harvard School of Geography, and two fellow students organized a two-month trip to the Clemenceau Icefield, approaching by the Athabasca River valley. Passing beneath the looming bulwark of Mount Columbia, Ostheimer and the party's Swiss guide, Hans Fuhrer, decided to make a reconnaissance of the Icefield above. After ascending the treacherous seracs of Columbia Glacier, the two men put a new route up North Twin, made first ascents of Mount Stutfield and Mount Kitchener, and completed the first traverse of Snow Dome – all in one continuous thirty-six hour burst of energy! And, had the weather not turned against them, they would have climbed Mount Columbia as well. During sixty-three days of wilderness travel the outfit amassed a total of 1040 kilometres and climbed thirty peaks, twenty-five of which were first ascents.

Of the 1920's Icefield visitors, the mountaineers were more vocal but fewer in number than the non-climbers. Timberline Kate's tours were often routed past the Icefield, and in 1924 a Banff outfit-

ter, Jack Brewster, began offering rides along "The Glacier Trail," six day journeys up the Bow, Mistaya, Alexandra, and Castleguard Rivers to the Castleguard Meadows. Jack's brother, Pat, started his own service, Brewster Mountain Pack Trains, in 1928, and on demand would run twenty day excursions to the meadows, allotting plenty of time for the dudes to hike, scramble, fish, and explore. The Trail Riders of the Canadian Rockies, an organization chartered in 1924 to promote horseback riding in the Rockies (and encourage use of the CPR's resorts), discovered the charms of the region on its 1929 outing.

Don's father, Byron Harmon, was an able climber, but his reason for including the Icefield on the itinerary of a seventy-day, eight hundred kilometre pack trip in 1924 was chiefly photographic. Travelling with an American writer, Lewis Freeman, Harmon hoped to photograph the mountains of the Columbia Icefield and shoot the first moving picture panorama of the Icefield from the summit of Mount Castleguard. It was a trip of unusual firsts: never before had anyone packed moving picture equipment to the Icefield, nor had anyone carried a radio and passenger pigeons into the region.

Freeman was interested in testing radio reception in the mountains (many thought there would be none), and Harmon pondered the ability of pigeons to find their way home through the tangle of peaks. The results were prophetic: the radio, despite much abuse by both pack horses and men, received the escalating babble of the twentieth-century in the wild core of the mountains, and the pigeons failed utterly to carry the message of the mountains to an increasingly complex civilization.

Of equal scientific insignificance was Freeman's discovery that glacial silt "had no equal...for putting on strops for sharpening razors." The silt, or *glacier flour,* is of a very fine particle size and is created at the base of the glacier as rock is dragged across rock under

tremendous pressure. Sharpening razors, Freeman noted, seemed to be its only redeeming attribute*: "The dust is so impalpable that it will filter through the closest woven canvas; the mud, at its worst, offers no resistance whatever to the downward passage of the foot or the body of horse or man."

The wrangler for the Harmon-Freeman expedition, Ulysses La Casse, affectionately known as Froggy (on account of his voice, broad grin, or French-Canadian ancestry, depending on the source), also made an interesting discovery on the trip. Accompanying the rest of the party on the climb of Mount Castleguard, La Casse fell unroped through a snow bridge and disappeared without a sound into a crevasse. Horrified, the other climbers turned toward the chasm, too stunned to act. In one split second a trusted friend and companion had vanished from the face of the earth. A terrible silence, an upwelling of grief–and Froggy suddenly burst from the mountainside far below, yipping and yahooing, shot from the far end of the crevasse like a cork from a champagne bottle. It's a far-fetched story, befitting the mountains, and likely more fanciful than factual since La Casse had done exactly the same thing in exactly the same place the year before with Thorington's outfit. Twice is sometimes once too often.

Harmon and Freeman headed back to Banff after a month at the Icefield, much satisfied with their adventure. Harmon had added over four hundred still photographs and seven thousand feet of movie footage to his collection, and Freeman had notes enough for a book on the journey.

From the days of the Icefield's discovery through the 1920's, activity at the Icefield was highly seasonal. If anything were to be accomplished, it had to be done between mid-June and mid-September. The new (to North America) pastime of skiing was becoming very popular by the mid-twenties, though, and it was natural for devotees to seek challenges commensurate with growing skills. Ever-longer trips, greater altitudes, and new territory are the passions of the backcountry skier, and in the Rockies of the late-twenties it was only a matter of time before someone began considering the snow-filled expanse between Jasper and Banff.

In March, 1932, Cliff White of Banff, Joe Weiss of Jasper, and Russell Bennett of Minneapolis, set out on a twenty-day, 480-kilometre run from Jasper to Banff. One of the highlights of their sub-zero spring frolic was a long day's side trip to the top of Snow Dome. White gave an account of the trip to the *Canadian Ski Annual,* where he reported that in sixteen hours of skiing,

> we had travelled thirty miles, climbed five thousand vertical feet of glacier slopes, and run down the same distance without stop...probably the most extensive and most spectacular ski descent possible in the Canadian Rockies.

His claims of the most extensive and most spectacular descent might be challenged today, but the spirit of the day's run was proven to be both endearing and enduring. Skis have become an indispensable aid for climbers attempting winter or spring ascents, and each winter many parties venture short distances up the Icefield's various tongues with no greater goal than to enjoy a little glacier skiing and scenery.

In 1933 White returned to the Icefield, using as part of his route a new, wide timber slash destined to have a significant impact on Icefield tourism. Late in 1931 survey and cutting crews started north from Lake Louise and south from Jasper, their goal to build a motor road between the two points.

As early as 1910 there was speculation as to the feasibility of a road, and a local story has it that Jimmy Simpson, upon first seeing Bow Lake in 1896, built himself a little cabin on the lakeshore and

---

*It does, in fact, have one other: the refractory qualities of the particles account for the wonderful turquoise colour of glacier-fed streams and lakes.

then settled in to wait for the tourists. Simpson couldn't have anticipated automobiles in 1896, but he knew a pretty spot when he saw one and realized that some future day a lot of people would be passing by. (By 1923 his little cabin had become Num-ti-jah Lodge, the intricate log edifice which still graces the shores of Bow Lake.)

The construction of the highway, supervised by the Department of the Interior, was an unemployment relief project and provided jobs for upward of six hundred men each year for the duration of the Depression. Tedious, dangerous, and physically demanding, the work occupied the better part of the decade. All the problems which had faced the packers of earlier years the road builders had to deal with anew. Muskeg, rock, forest, sidehill, cliff, and swift water had to be filled, blasted, cleared, or bridged to produce a uniform forty-foot right-of-way with a maximum six-percent grade. Much of the initial work, which involved scratching a mountain "toe-hold" for bulldozers and graders, was done entirely by hand—all for twenty cents a day, plus room and board. Provisions came in by tractor and sleigh in winter and by pack train and truck in summer.

Upon its completion (the official opening was June 15, 1940), the Banff-Jasper Highway was hailed an engineering and construction marvel. Even the New York *Times* took notice. Gravelled, with an oil surface, the road was deemed both "safe"—for the reasonable driver—and "spectacular" by the daring feature writers who ventured onto the "Highway in the Clouds."

Highway access altered completely the nature of sight-seeing at the Columbia Icefield. What had previously been a rugged four to five day trail ride was suddenly a comfortable, if exciting, drive of four to five hours. The Brewster family proved adaptable by trading in some of its pack horses for buses (which they had been using in Banff since the 1920's), and by winning a tender from the Parks Service to operate a visitors' lodge at the Icefield. The Athabasca

Chalet, precursor of the present Columbia Icefield Chalet, opened its doors the same summer the road was completed, and the staff soon learned the sensibilities, if not priorities, of the motoring public differed considerably from those of the old horse set. One motorist, highly vexed upon learning the chalet served no mixed drinks, pointed across the road to the Athabasca snout and muttered, "All that ice, and it's no damned good!"

Within three years of its opening, the chalet became a quite different type of lodge than the one its builders envisaged. As World War Two became a truly global conflict, it was obvious that battles would eventually be fought in mountainous terrain. The Allies, realizing their armies were unprepared to deal with such contingencies, took steps to train selected troops to operate in high mountains.

The Canadian Rockies provided a natural setting for the training, and in October of 1943 the Canadian Army, in conjunction with the British Army, conducted a pilot course to select eight instructors. It was little coincidence that many of those chosen were men from the nearby western mountain communities. In January, 1944, eight hundred Lovat Scouts, a battalion composed largely of soldiers from northern Scotland, and two hundred Canadian Army personnel arrived in Jasper to be dispersed in smaller units to six different training areas in the Jasper vicinity. Two hundred of the men were billeted at the Athabasca Chalet.

The program seemed simple enough on paper, but the instructors were quick to recognize some serious shortcomings. Although many of the Lovat Scouts were good marksmen and tough highland gillies with previous rock climbing experience, few of them knew the difference between a ski and a crevasse. The instructors had but a scant six weeks to teach rank novices the considerable intricacies of skiing, winter mountaineering, mountain rescue, and cold weather survival. The process was complicated by the troop officers, remembered by an instructor as the sort who would take their golf clubs into battle. It was infuriating to both students and instructors for one of these gentlemen officers–quickly more ignorant of the mountains than were the men they commanded–to trace an impossible route on a map, name it as the day's operation, and then turn back to fire and pantry while the enlisted men donned parkas and skis.

It was, though, a time most participants remember fondly.* A totally new environment and the acquisition of new skills were great stimuli for those involved. Only one fatality occurred in the entire program; one of the Scouts was killed by an avalanche. The record is remarkable when one considers the inexperience of the trainees and the severe nature of the training. Troops at the Icefield claimed the first winter ascents of Mounts Columbia, Kitchener, Andromeda, and Nigel Peak.

Although the training was intensive there was time for rest and relaxation, and the Scouts were noted for their parties. One instructor remembers stumbling out of the chalet one evening for a breath of fresh air and seeing–in a black, snow-choked, windy night–a Scout in full kilts staggering out across the snow toward Athabasca Glacier, bagpipes wailing a drunken obligato for mountain blizzard.

A cheerless and ironic footnote to the story of the Lovat Scouts: the battalion failed to survive long enough to see the sort of action for which it was trained. Suffering over two hundred casualties during the early part of the invasion of Italy, The Scouts, as a unit, perished far from any mountain.

The American Army, a year earlier, had also found use for the Icefield. In the summer of 1942, forty-five members of the Eighty-seventh Mountain Division established a camp near the snout of Saskatchewan Glacier. Using the glacier as a proving ground for army vehicles, the men drove an armada of jeeps, trucks, half-tracks, and snowmobiles across the tongue, grading roads and bridging crevasses. One wonders what Collie would have thought had he known of the successful ascent by vehicle of Snow Dome, not to mention the landing of a Norseman plane on its flanks. The Icefield claimed at least part of its own back by swallowing a jeep.

Corrugated metal huts and camp tents were erected at several points along the glacier, including one hut high on the Divide. Today's glacier hikers are forcefully reminded of the war effort as they stumble onto the tin cans, crates, wooden timbers, faded signs, and spools of wire which litter segments of the glacier's face. Supplied by truck, the men in the high camps lived a life of "style and comfort" on the ice until late fall. It seems unfortunate, in light of today's zero impact environmental ethic, that the Americans should have been so negligent with their garbage as the last trucks rumbled off the ice.

If the history of the Columbia Icefield is viewed as a history of three eras–exploration, mountaineering, and visitation–the post-war period can be seen as a special sub-era, a time of high density visitation. The Banff-Jasper Highway was reconstructed and resurfaced between 1955 and 1962, largely a response to the burgeoning number of post-war tourists, and today more than three-quarters of a million people pass by the Athabasca tongue each year. (In order to avoid the sticky question of whether the road was actually the Banff-Jasper, or the Jasper-Banff, Highway–a touchy, if decidedly silly point of contention between the two rival communities–the road was renamed the Icefields Parkway in the seventies.) The snowmobile concession, begun in 1948 when a man named Alex Watt slapped a half-track on an old Brewster bus and drove it up the Athabasca toe,

*One possible exception would be the memories of a soldier involved in a summer mountaineering exercise in Yoho National Park. Reaching the summit of his first mountain he scanned the horizon and said: "Imagine asking a man to fight for a country like this. I'd *give* it all to the Japs!"

Snowmobile, Athabasca Glacier, c. 1945

today consists of a fleet of some twenty Bombardier and Foremost snow machines. On a good day three thousand sight-seers take the forty-minute, four-kilometre run up the tongue. Dozens of tour buses drive the Parkway each day of the summer, and the Columbia Icefield Chalet does its best to accommodate the hundreds of hungry, thirsty, and curious tourists that pass through it every day. Parks Canada, following decades of what can best be described as paternalistic non-policy management, opened its interpretive centre in 1973, and in the last years of the seventies decided to expand and upgrade its Icefield programme, committing funds for improved hiking trails, increased staff, and a more comprehensive interpretive display at the visitors' centre.

Despite the massive tourism, the spirit of exploration and mountaineering adventure lives on. The Parkway, after all, is only a road on the valley floor, and the Athabasca tongue but one tongue of many. Mysteries still abound. Until 1967, for instance, no one had been further into the Castleguard Cave than the W.O. Field party of 1924. It remains a riddle today, and the story of its ongoing investigation possesses all the romance and intrigue of the grand explorations of the late 1890's. Two members of the 1967 exploratory party, returning to the entrance after an eighteen hour journey into the cave's recesses, found their exit blocked by a flood of the sort which had led to the cave's discovery forty-three years before. With no carbide for their lamps, no food, and, seemingly, no future, the men shivered through several hours entombed before the water subsided and let them pass. After five hours it began to rise again, and two other members of the party who had entered the cave to retrieve equipment escaped at the last minute by floating through the final chamber on their backs with their noses pressed against the rough limestone ceiling. The water didn't fall again for eighteen days.

Hot weather run-off drains into the lower levels of the cave to feed a spring which issues from the mountainside a short distance below the cave entrance. Whenever the amount of run-off exceeds the amount the spring can discharge, water wells up into the lower passage of the cave. The flooding is both violent and unpredictable, making caving a hazardous undertaking in all but the winter months, and Parks Canada fenced off the portals in 1975 to protect the unwary.

Since 1967 there have been repeated expeditions into the cave, subterranean wanderings of a duration and hardship to match the early climbs on Mount Columbia and the Twins. In the spring of 1980 an international expedition of twenty-five explorers spent ten days prying the cave, hoping, as the group's leader, Derek Ford, put it, "to finish the darn thing off." They came close to achieving their goal, but even after amassing a total of 1,700 man hours in the cave they

88

found themselves short of time to follow all the possible leads.*

Mountaineering remains a popular pastime at the Icefield. No sooner has the last of the Icefield summits been attained than a new generation of climbers began to put different, more difficult routes up the same peaks. In August, 1970, in a two and a half day epic, two of the new breed of "iron men," C. Jones and G. Thompson, completed what the alpinists of the last century would have considered impossible: an ascent of the north face of Mount Columbia. In yet more recent years climbers skilled in technical rock and ice work have scaled the tremendously difficult and desperately dangerous northwest faces of Mount Kitchener and Snow Dome, raising the ante of their game by making the ascents in winter.

The future? The complexity of glacial cycles is such that no one can predict with certainty what lies ahead for the great white beasts. Surely no scientist alive will promise they shall not stir and creep forth from their mountain fastnesses to dominate the land and its life once more. In that doubt exists an admonition for us all. Loren Eiseley, the great American anthropologist and writer who died in 1977, expressed it most clearly:

> These fractured mementoes of devastating cold need to be contemplated for another reason than themselves. They constitute exteriorly what may be contemplated interiorly. They contain a veiled warning, perhaps the greatest symbolic warning man has ever received from nature. The giant fragments whisper, in the words of Einstein, that 'nature does not always play the same game.'**

High above the mountain wall, oblivious to the science and the secret aspirations of man, the sleeping dragons lie, waiting...

*Eiseley, Loren. "The Winter of Man," in *The Star Thrower.* New York: Harcourt Brace Jovanovich, 1978.

**Professor Ford's account of the expedition, along with conclusions concerning the existence of Castleguard II, the cave believed to be running somewhere far beneath Castleguard Cave, can be found in *Canadian Geographic* magazine, Volume 100, No. 4, August-September, 1980.

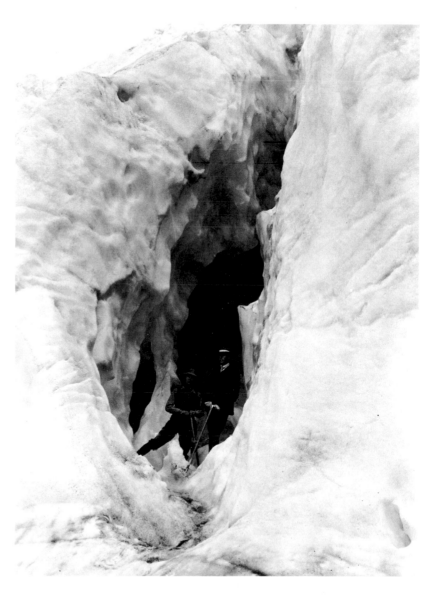

Two men in a crevasse, 1924

Only a few months ago came a letter from Fred (Stephens) saying: 'I know of some valleys hidden away, where the beavers still build their lodges, and where there are fish in the streams, and wild raspberries, and cariboo. Say, friend, come! and let the whole dam world race for dollars.'

J.N. Collie, 1923

Sunrise on Mount Athabasca

Freezing meltwater,
Athabasca Glacier

Broken ice and
suncups,
Athabasca Glacier

Crevasses, unnamed glacier,
western margins
of the Columbia Icefield

Mount Castleguard (foreground) and Mount Bryce from the head of Saskatchewan Glacier

96

Tongue, Columbia Glacier

Icefall, Stutfield Glacier

Snow Dome and the northeast margin of the Columbia Icefield

GLOSSARY

Ablation The wastage or weathering away of a glacier, chiefly by melt and evaporation.

Ablation Zone The portion of a glacier lying below the equilibrium line where more snow wastes away during the course of a year than accumulates. Also known as the wastage, or melt zone.

Accumulation Zone The portion of a glacier lying above the equilibrium line where more snow accumulates during the course of a year than wastes away.

Bergschrund A crevasse separating the moving ice of a glacier and the stationary ice and snow clinging to a rock wall or headwall of a valley.

Cirque A three-sided bowl or amphitheatre, often of great dimension, carved by a glacier from the side of a mountain.

Crevasse A fissure transecting a glacier's surface and formed by various stresses in the glacier mantle.

Firn Metamorphosed snow. An intermediary stage between snow and ice, firn is characterized by the fact that the individual grains have to some extent joined together, but that the air pores between grains still connect, or communicate.

Glacier A body of perennial ice which forms in those areas of the world where more snow accumulates than melts or evaporates. The ice must show evidence of flow before it is considered a glacier.

Glacier Ice A dense, impermeable polycrystalline mineral composed of ice crystals and air bubbles. It is characterized by the fact that the air pores between ice granules are sealed off from each other and no longer communicate.

Equilibrium Line The line or zone on a glacier where a year's ablation balances a year's accumulation of snowfall.

Icefall A portion of a glacier flowing over a steep reach of bedrock. An icefall will exhibit a steep gradient, extensive crevassing, and many seracs.

Icefield An ice mass with the appearance of a blanket or sheet and which reflects, in form and flow, the irregularities of the underlying bedrock.

Karst A type of topography generated as water containing carbon dioxide dissolves formations of limestones, dolomite, or gypsum. It is characterized by sinkholes, caves, and extensive underground drainage systems.

Mill Hole A vertical hole penetrating the glacier mantle which funnels meltwater streams into the interior of the glacier. Mill holes are found in the ablation zone of a glacier. Also known as *moulins* and *glacier mills*.

Moraine Any rock debris transported or deposited by a glacier. The rock may be carried on top of, within, or beneath the moving ice and results in a number of depositional features.

Névé See *Firn*. Névé is also occasionally used to designate the accumulation zone of an icefield.

Ogives Alternating dark and light bands, or waves, of ice forming a distinct, repetitive convex downstream pattern across a glacier tongue. They are thought to be caused by the seasonal passage of ice down a steep icefall.

Outlet Glacier Any ice stream issuing from a glacier source.

Randkluft The moat separating the moving ice of a glacier from a rock wall.

Regenerated Glacier A glacier formed and nourished by ice which has broken free of, and fallen from, an ice source somewhere above. Also called a reconstituted glacier.

Snowline The ragged line across a glacier tongue which marks the summer's melt of snow deposited during the previous winter. An ephemeral feature, the line moves progressively upglacier as the summer progresses. At its maximum altitude it is known as the annual snowline.

Serac A pillar or spire of ice formed by the intersection of crevasses.

Terminus The leading (downvalley) edge of a glacier tongue. Also known as the glacier toe, or snout.

Tongue The main body of an outlet glacier.

Valley Glacier Any glacier occupying a well-defined valley.

Wastage Zone See ablation zone.

SUGGESTED READING LIST

Natural History

Baranowski, S., W.E.S. Henoch and R.E. Kucera. *Glacier and Landform Features in the Columbia Icefield Area, Banff and Jasper National Parks, Alberta, Canada.* Ottawa: Inland Waters Directorate, 1978.

Dyson, James L. *The World of Ice.* New York: Alfred A Knopf, 1962.

Harrison, A.E. *Exploring Glaciers.* San Francisco: Sierra Club, 1960.

Ines, J.D. "Glaciers," in *Geomorphology* (ed. Chambers, M.J., and J.G. Nelson). Toronto: Methuen, 1969.

Kucera, R.E. *Probing the Athabasca Glacier.* Vancouver: Evergreen Press, 1972.

LaChapelle, Edward R., and Austin Post. *Glacier Ice.* Seattle: University of Washington Press, 1971.

Paterson, W.S.B. *The Physics of Glaciers.* Toronto: Premagon Books, 1969.

Sharp, Robert S. *Glaciers.* Eugene, Oregon: University of Oregon Press, 1960.

Readers interested in yet more information may want to obtain C. Simon L. Ommanney's bibliography, "Information Relating to Glaciers of the Columbia Icefield Area, Banff and Jasper National Parks, Alberta." It is a 1976 internal report of the Glaciology Division, Environment Canada.

Human History

Coleman, A.P. *The Canadian Rockies, Old and New Trails.* London: T. Fisher Unwin, 1911.

Collie, J.N., and H.E.M. Stutfield. *Climbs and Explorations in the Canadian Rockies.* London: Longmans, Green and Co., 1903.

Fraser, Esther. *The Canadian Rockies: Early Travels and Explorations.* Edmonton: M.G. Hurtig Ltd., 1969.

Freeman, Lewis R. *On the Roof of the Rockies.* New York: Dodd, Mead and Company, 1925.

Harmon, Carole (ed.) *Great Days in the Rockies: The Photographs of Byron Harmon, 1906-1934.* Toronto: Oxford University Press, 1978.

Hart, E.J. *Diamond Hitch.* Banff: Summerthought, 1979.

Kain, Conrad. *Where the Clouds Can Go* (ed. J.M. Thorington). New York: The American Alpine Club, 1935.

Outram, James. *In the Heart of the Canadian Rockies.* New York: MacMillan & Company, 1925.

Schäffer, Mary T.S. *Old Indian Trails of the Canadian Rockies.* New York: Putnam & Son, 1911.

Taylor, William G. *The Snows of Yesteryear: J. Norman Collie, Mountaineer.* Toronto: Holt, Rinehart and Winston of Canada, Ltd., 1973.

Thorington, J.M. *The Glittering Mountains of Canada.* Philadelphia: John Lea, 1925.

Wilcox, W.D. *The Rockies of Canada.* New York: G.P. Putnam's Sons, 1900.

The Alpine Journal, American Alpine Journal, *and* Canadian Alpine Journal *are highly recommended to students of human activity in the Canadian Rockies.*

Mountain Metaphysics

Clark, Ronald. *The Victorian Mountaineers.* London: B.T. Batsford Ltd., 1953.

Jerome, John. Chapter 1, in *On Mountains.* New York: McGraw-Hill, 1978.

Nicolson, Marjorie Hope. *Mountain Gloom and Mountain Glory: The Development of the Aesthetics of the Infinite.* New York: W.W. Norton, 1963.

Noyce, Wilfred. *Scholar Mountaineers.* London: Dennis Dobson, 1949.

APPENDIX

Appendix: *Columbia Icefield Peaks over 3350 Metres*

MOUNTAIN	HEIGHT	FIRST ASCENT	NAMED BY	NAMED FOR
Mount Columbia[1]	3747.2	1902; J. Outram, C. Kaufmann	J.N. Collie, H. Woolley, H. Stutfield	Columbia River
North Twin[2]	3683.5	1923; W.S. Ladd, J.M. Thorington C. Kain	J.N. Collie, H. Woolley, H. Stutfield	Topographical Appearance
South Twin	3558.5	1924; F.V. Field, W.O. Field, L. Harris, J. Biner, E. Feuz, Jr.	J.N. Collie, H. Woolley, H. Stutfield	Topographical Appearance
Mount Bryce	3507.3	1902; J. Outram, C. Kaufmann	J.N. Collie, H. Woolley, H. Stutfield	James Bryce, president, Alpine Club
Mount Kitchener	3505.2	1927; A.J. Ostheimer, H. Fuhrer	Geographical Board of Canada	Horatio Herbert, First Earl Kitchener of Khartoum and of Broome
Mount Athabasca	3490.5	1898; J.N. Collie, H. Woolley	J.N. Collie, H. Woolley, H. Stutfield	Athabasca River
Mount King Edward	3474.7	1924; J. Hickson, H. Palmer, C. Kain	A. Carpe, H. Palmer	King Edward VII
Snow Dome	3456.4	1898; J.N. Collie, H. Stutfield, H. Woolley	J.N. Collie, H. Woolley, H. Stutfield	Topographical Appearance
Stutfield Peak[3]	3450.3	1927; A.J. Ostheimer, H. Fuhrer	J.N. Collie, H. Woolley, H. Stutfield	H. Stutfield, British alpinist
Mount Andromeda	3444.2	1930; W.R. Hainsworth, J.F. Lehman, M.M. Strumia, N.D. Waffl	Rex Gibson	Wife of Perseus in Greek Mythology

[1]Highest peak of the Icefield environs, second elevation of the Canadian Rockies.
[2]Third elevation of the Canadian Rockies and first elevation entirely within Alberta's borders.
[3]Originally named Mount Douglas by Collie, Stutfield, and Woolley.

LIST OF PLATES

THE PHOTOGRAPHER Don Harmon is a native of the Canadian Rockies. He was born in 1917 and raised in Banff. At the outset of World War II he joined the R.C.A.F. and spent the war years as a flight navigator stationed in Britain. Following the war he returned to the Rockies with his war bride, Norah, and joined the family business, Byron Harmon Photos, continuing the tradition of photographing and publishing classic views of the Rocky Mountains.

THE WRITER Bart Robinson, raised and educated in the United States, moved to Canada in 1968 at the age of 22. He has been studying and writing about the natural and human history of the Canadian Rockies for the past 11 years. His previous publications include: *Banff Springs, the Story of a Hotel, The Canadian Rockies Trail Guide* (co-author), *Great Days in the Rockies* (co-author), and he is a regular contributor to several outdoor magazines. He lives in Canmore, Alberta with his wife, Susan Beckett, and their child.

text editor   *Jon Whyte*
photography editor   *Carole Harmon*
original art for maps on pp. 17 and 67   *Stephen Hutchings*

design   *Scott Thornley*
art production   *Glynn Bell*
typesetting   *Crocker Bryant Inc.*
colour separations   *Prolith Inc.*
printing   *Proving Specialties Ltd.*